Practical Suggestions for Hopeful Missionaries

By
Erik Stapleton

The maps of Vanuatu and Tanna Island in the front of the book © 2014 by JohnMark Stapleton.

Unless otherwise specified all scripture quotations are from the NIV version © 1984.

This book is copyright. Apart from any fair dealing for the purpose of private study, research, criticism or review as permitted under the Copyright Act, no part of this publication may be reproduced, stored in a retrieval system, or transmitted in any form or by any means electronic, mechanical, photocopying, recording or otherwise without prior written permission.

First edition
© 2014 by Erik Stapleton

ISBN – 13: 978-1495225000
ISBN – 10: 1495225003

This book is lovingly dedicated to those tireless, servant-hearted people who made the South Tanna Translation & Literacy Project happen each day for a decade. May the Lord remember your commitment and endurance. May he cause your friends and neighbors to understand more clearly the gospel message because you have worked so hard to translate it into your heart language, and may it change their lives for eternity through Jesus Christ!

To Tata Nato, David Nasu, Alan Raui, Nekkie Mahu, Jimmy Nato, Nettie Dan, Joseph Narkahau (not pictured) and the communities of Ienmarei, Kwamera, Kwaraka, Itaku, Port Resolution, Neprai Netata, Imaki, Imwanier, and Greenpoint

Contents

Maps
Introduction

PART ONE

Chapter One
Conversion and Becoming Interested in Fulltime Service

Chapter Two
Preparation at Moody Bible Institute

Chapter Three
My First Year Overseas -- Heartsick

Chapter Four
Introduction to Tanna

PART TWO

Chapter Five
Axiom One: Maintain Your Spiritual Vitality

Chapter Six
Axiom Two: Know the Culture

Chapter Seven
Axiom Three: Don't Offend Unnecessarily

Chapter Eight
Axiom Four: Avoid the Gospel-For-Profit Perception

Chapter Nine
Axiom Five: Make Incarnational Ministry Your Goal

Chapter Ten
Axiom Six -- Love People by Eating Their Food

Chapter Eleven
Axiom Seven -- Avoid Being Ethnocentric

Chapter Twelve
Axiom Eight -- Learn to Laugh at Yourself

Chapter Thirteen
Axiom Nine -- Keep Your Marriage Strong

Chapter Fourteen
Axiom Ten -- Trust in God's Sovereignty

Chapter Fifteen
Conclusion: Missions Possible!

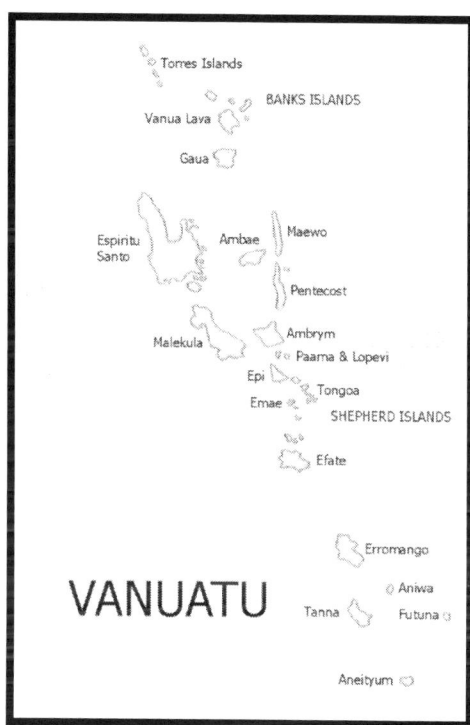

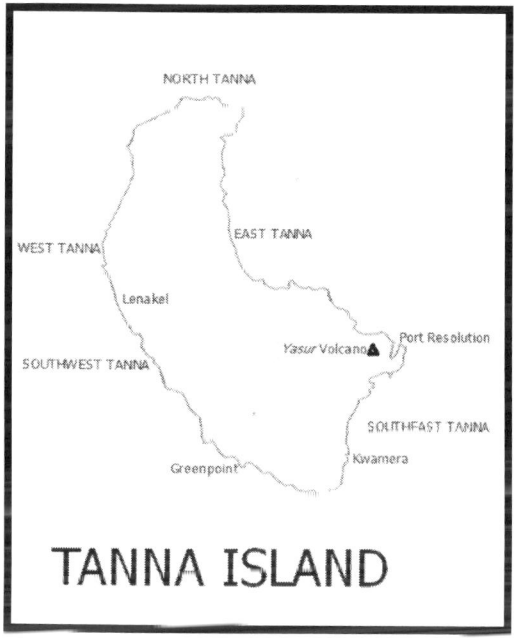

Introduction

My name is Erik Stapleton. My wife's name is Michele. We have four children: JohnMark (1998), Sierra (1999), David (2000), and Joel (2005). Michele and I are both members of Wycliffe Bible Translators and have been since the summer we graduated from Moody Bible Institute in 1998. From 2001 until the present (Jan. 2013), we have lived overseas in Vanuatu, an archipelago comprised of eighty-plus islands in the South Pacific. We have spent ten years in TAFEA Province, which is located in the southern part of the nation. The "T" in the acronym stands for Tanna, the island we call our home. We live on the southeastern side of the island in an isolated village occupied by ~120 people.

We work among the ~3500 *Nafe* speakers. The eastern border of the *Nafe* language group is Port Resolution; the southern border is Greenpoint village. The speakers of *Nafe* are Melanesian. It's worth pointing out only because a neighboring island is inhabited by Polynesians.

Several years ago during our first four years on Tanna I had made the two-hour journey around the island to the modest town named Lenakel. It was hot. I was standing outside the post office waiting for it to open. I was happy when I saw another foreigner milling around in the crowd. I walked over to him and struck up a conversation. It turned out he and his wife were just passing through on the tail end of yachting season on their way to Fiji. I'll call the man Brad.

Brad and I made small talk for several minutes. I asked him about the work he had done before retiring to his yacht. We talked about the weather and the upcoming cyclone season. We chatted about his home on the west coast of the United States. Then the conversation turned to the inevitable question:

"So what do you do on Tanna?" Brad asked.

"What is your religious background?" I replied.

He looked at me with a puzzled expression. I could tell from his eyes he was wondering what in the world his religious background had to do with anything. "I'm an agnostic," he finally said. "I didn't grow up with religion, and I've never seen any need for it."

I nodded. Although Brad would probably be polite, I knew he wouldn't be able to appreciate what I was doing on Tanna. Nonetheless, I burped it out: "I'm a missionary. I work as a translation advisor in the language spoken in Southeast Tanna with a committee formed by the Christian churches there. We are translating the New Testament and running a vernacular literacy program."

Brad seemed surprised. "Really?" he said. He was quiet for several seconds and then added, "How did you get interested in that sort of work?"

On that particular occasion I didn't go into great detail about my personal, spiritual motivation for Bible translation and literacy. I kept it general, speaking about the many undeveloped languages in the world. I told him about how I had studied Bible and was pursuing an MA in linguistics.

My conversation with Brad that day has been multiplied innumerable times over the years as I've met and conversed with many non-sympathetic people from the First World. These people's curiosity has always compelled them to ask why exactly my family and I left behind the United States with all its perceived advantages in order to settle for a decade on a remote island. After all, the First World is a place where a person with a little ingenuity can become a millionaire. Why did I leave all that behind and move with my children to a place where people can be found on a regular basis sitting together picking lice from one another's hair and killing them between their teeth?

When I talk with people about my work as a fulltime Christian missionary, most of them act like Brad. They smile and listen politely, although I know if they were honest they would admit that they think I'm wasting my time while robbing my children of their opportunity to get ahead. The odd person will disagree with the task. The man who suggested Christian evangelism and Bible translation will ruin the local culture comes to mind. Another guffawed among his friends, "Wow, I'm surprised missionaries still exist."

It's true most people won't be able to understand or appreciate what motivated me to became a fulltime Christian missionary, but there are some who can. There are many young people who understand in a personal way the missionary's motivation because they feel it burning in their own hearts. Some are still in high school. Others are in college or at the age where they could attend. These are the individuals that have motivated me to write this book.

If you are a young person who wants to be a missionary, and yet you have many questions that fill you with apprehension or uncertainty, I want to encourage you by sharing my own story. Is becoming a missionary possible? How do I pursue such a course?

Where will I serve? How will I get there? What principles will help me become successful working in a cross-cultural context? I invite you to see how these questions were answered in my own life, and I pray reading about them will benefit you in your own journey.

This book is neither scientific nor exhaustive. If I make missiological assertions, they are from my experience in a single part of the world, namely, an animistic culture in the South Pacific. I don't intend to suggest they are true everywhere on the globe and in all situations.

I've divided this book into two parts. In Part One I give a brief description of my own background, focusing on my testimony and how my interest in fulltime Christian missions was first developed. I continue by telling the story of my pre-field years, including the years of training and deciding upon the place where we would serve. My first year overseas gets its own chapter. I discuss briefly the island of Tanna. I share all these things while offering practical suggestions at the end of each chapter. Part Two is a lengthier section wherein I discuss ten helpful axioms applicable to the missionary working in a cross-cultural environment.

May God use these meager efforts to help prepare young people to spread his matchless reputation to distant lands.

PART ONE

CHAPTER ONE

CONVERSION AND BECOMING INTERESTED IN FULLTIME SERVICE

Many Christian young people struggle within themselves as they contemplate whether or not they should become fulltime Christian missionaries serving overseas. Part of their struggle arises because they assume such a vocation requires a divine call, and they are not sure they have one. They reason that being a foreign missionary is a bit like being a prophet, and we all know the prophets received a special call, right! After all, Moses saw a burning bush. Samuel heard a voice in the night. Isaiah caught a glimpse of the Lord high and lifted up. Ezekiel saw a vision of God's glory atop a flaming throne on wheels. Then there was the apostle Paul in the New Testament thrown to the ground and blinded by a heavenly light.

While some people struggle with the question of calling, I never have. Deciding to become a fulltime Christian missionary was a natural, easy choice for me. It grew out of my conversion experience which occurred over twenty-two years ago when I was nineteen years old. In order to understand what happened to me at that time, I need to take you back there with me. But first a little background information.

My father's family is from Irish stock. My great-great grandfather, Timothy, immigrated to the United States from Ireland in the mid 1800s. He was a Presbyterian in religious belief and eventually ended up in Aspen, Colorado, where he settled a large homestead. His son, my great-grandfather, was the father of five boys, one of them my father's dad, Elmer.

Grandpa Elmer left Aspen and settled in Denver after fighting in the Pacific War during World War II. He used to visit his old home regularly and my father learned to hunt, fish, and get around in the wild from Grandpa Elmer and his relatives. Unfortunately, my father's family was just as avid about drinking alcohol as they were about their hunting. I remember many family reunions where the drinking started early and by late afternoon the partying would be out of hand.

Mom's story was different. The oldest of five, she grew up in a stable, religious home. This meant she attended Mass every Sunday, carefully kept the religious holidays, and attended Catholic school first through seventh grades. However, the Bible wasn't something she read or was taught, and a personal relationship with Jesus Christ wasn't emphasized.

Dad and Mom met and married young before having a chance to finish college. My older brother was born a year later, and soon after his birth my dad was drafted into the U.S. Army. It was late 1970 and the war in Vietnam was still being fought. The family ended up in Fort Rucker, Alabama, and that's where I was born. I was three months premature and born on my brother's second birthday.

After 18 months, my father's time in the military ended. We returned to our home in Colorado. Dad went back to his work as a glazier. We bought our first house and settled down. Dad worked hard each day, but alcohol remained an important, harmful habit he held onto in the evenings.

On the weekends my whole family could be found up in the mountains near Fairplay, an old gold-mining town. We had property there and regularly camped, fished, and enjoyed the outdoors. Sundays were sacred for either watching the Denver Broncos on the television or listening to them on the radio. September through January was hunting season. We pursued elk and deer first and then ducks and geese. That was our life, and it was exciting and fun as a child.

My grandparents on my father's side were killed in a car accident when I was six. This was a very difficult time for my parents, and my mother began to question her religion. As God would have it, a new neighbor moved in right at that time. I remember her well. She was a happy, gregarious, African-American woman named Irene. She loved Jesus and was happy to share her faith with everyone in the cul-de-sac where we lived.

To make a long story short, through Irene's friendship, Mom became a born-again Christian. She prayed fervently for Dad for two years, and the Lord was gracious and eventually changed his heart, too. Dad made a confession of faith when I was eight. The whole family began attending a large Christian Missionary Alliance church in our neighborhood. My brother and I were baptized and began attending Awanas. Mom became more and more involved with church activities. Dad got involved in Evangelism Explosion.

Regular church attendance was short lived in my family. After a couple years we stopped going except on holidays. My parents began to fight more often. Mom became depressed. Dad started drinking again. They sought professional counseling, which in the end the Lord used to help them develop some new, healthy habits. (They have been happily married now for four and a half decades because of His grace in their lives.)

During my tumultuous teenage years I was left to do whatever I wanted. I ditched school, went from house to house visiting friends who weren't Christians, and watched lots of what I now consider destructive television and movies. Most of it glorified casual sex and other unwholesome lifestyle choices. Sadly, I watched volumes of such entertainment without conscience as a young man. I was unaware of the strong, negative influence it had on my unguarded heart. No one had reminded me of Jesus' warning:

> Woe to the world because of the things that cause people to sin! Such things must come, but woe to the man through whom they come! If your hand or your foot causes you to sin, cut it off and throw it away. It's better for you to enter life maimed or crippled than to have two hands or two feet and be thrown into eternal fire. And if your eye causes you to sin, gouge it out and throw it away. It's better for you to enter life with one eye than to have two eyes than to be thrown into the fire of hell (Matt. 18:7-9).

In high school, I didn't excel at academics. So, instead of taking classes in advanced math and science, I chose weight training, auto mechanics, and half-days at the off-campus trade school learning photography. I worked every afternoon at a cable building company and used the money I earned to finance bicycle racing, which was a positive hobby I enjoyed for a couple years.

    I graduated in 1990 with neither money nor desire for college. I talked with my older brother about the military. He had joined the U.S. Marines the year before and encouraged me to join the U.S. Air Force because the food was better. I took his advice and found myself two months later in basic training at Lackland Air Force Base in San Antonio, Texas.

    When I left home the summer after graduating from high school, I was 6'1 and weighed 190 solid pounds, the result of countless hours working out with a buddy in his basement gym. Outwardly I fit in well with the other young men in my squadron. I could certainly cuss up a storm with the rest of them and stay with the leaders of the pack during physical training. On the inside, however, I was hurting because of a broken heart. (While in basic training my high school sweetheart informed me she had met a guy at the movies and they had decided to marry.)

    I made it through my first six weeks in San Antonio. After finishing basic training there, I was sent down to Biloxi, Mississippi, where I began school to become an air traffic controller. I was there four months total. During that time, by God's grace, I not only began learning a totally new skill, but I also survived Mardi Gras in New Orleans and the hostility of Biloxi's young men who didn't really appreciate the out-of-town boys from the military base on their doorstep competing for the affection of their young ladies.

    When the time came for me to receive orders, I was assigned

to a base in England. At that point in my life I couldn't have pointed to England on a map. All I knew was it was a foreign country and far away from home. Help came with Airman Omale. I still recall her name after 20-plus years because of the great relief I felt when she communicated the same dismay over her orders. All the places in the world and she had been assigned to Alaska! While she imagined the worst, I had visions of hunting big game and salmon fishing. It took us less than five minutes and we agreed to a swap.

I arrived at Eielson AFB outside of Fairbanks, Alaska, in the early months of 1991. It was cold and dark, worlds away from anything I had ever experienced. The way the northern lights danced across the frigid, starry sky was surreal, a silent reminder of the creativity of the God I still didn't know personally. The snow drifts never seemed to melt, rising higher and higher. Highways buckled and cracked under the pressure of the ground which expanded as it froze. I felt like there couldn't be another place like it on earth. It was both scary and beautiful at the same time.

Eielson AFB had one runway nearly three miles long. It was the home of two squadrons of F-16 fighters, several A-10 tank killers that had been instrumental in the Gulf War, and a squadron of KC-135 refueling planes. My primary duty station was in the control tower. I began training immediately, working in partnership with experienced controllers until I would become competent enough to get certified to work solo in any of the tower's three control positions.

One of my workmates was a Christian. Knowing I was new, he reached out to me in the same way Irene had reached out to my mother years before. He asked me to join him for church on the following Sunday. I agreed, thinking at the time it would be a good place to find a nice girl to date.

I did meet a female at that church service. Her name was Katcha, a fifty-something Turkish woman whose attempts at dying her hair had left long streaks of purple. When the service was over, she came up to me and introduced herself. She was holding a copy of *The NIV Study Bible* in her hand. She gave it to me and said, "The Lord put it on my heart to purchase this for you. This is God's word. Take it home. Read it and study it."

Looking back, Alaska was a perfect Egypt for me, a place where I felt God was protecting me and preparing me for something he had planned for me in the future. Had I gone to England, I wonder if I would have taken the time to read either the Bible or any book for that matter. But Alaska! What's a person supposed to do during the cold, dark, long days and nights of winter if not read? So that is what I did, and there in my dorm room while I poured over the sacred words of Scripture I was convicted of my sins and born again by God's grace through faith alone in His Son.

After trusting in Christ, I started attending a Grace Brethren church near the base. The pastor began teaching me how to study the Bible inductively. His family opened their home to me like I was their son. The resident missionary, an old, energetic man with the Bible League who used to make trips back and forth to Russia took me under his wing and allowed me to help him distribute food and Bibles around town.

I also got involved with LOVE Inc., or Love In the Name of Christ. This was a ministry reaching out to the homeless and needy in the Fairbanks area. In response to calls made on the phone my friends and I would do acts of kindness in Jesus' name. We would deliver boxes of food to the hungry, shovel heavy snow for widows, visit dying people in the hospital, and sometimes attempt to talk sense with homeless men and women who had had too much to drink.

I attended an outreach of Cadence International, a ministry designed for single servicemen from both the army base in town and Eielson where I was stationed. The staff missionary, Craig, had graduated from Moody Bible Institute and became a close friend. He had us over for meals once a week and on holidays. He led Bible studies, took us on camping trips, and encouraged us immensely in our spiritual growth.

One memorable moment illustrating the sort of one-on-one discipleship Craig engaged in took place underneath the servicemen's center one summer afternoon. I had come over in my off hours to give him a hand with the clogged plumbing. We were lying in the crawl space. It was hot and smelly, the kind of situation that would have elicited loud shouts of profanity had I still been in my pre-Christ condition. Craig turned a pipe this way or that, revealing an undesirable cesspool. Just when I expected a string of profanity, he let out a loud laugh and turned his face toward me in a grimace. "Blech, Erik, there's nothing better to test your sanctification than the plumbing!"

I experienced many other memorable moments at the servicemen's center. One year I went to Okinawa, Japan, for the Cadence International annual conference. As I met various staff members who were engaged in discipling servicemen around the world, it helped me recognize the global mission of the Church.

Concerning that global mission, I was at the servicemen's center in Alaska when I saw for the first time a video produced by New Tribes Mission (NTM). I hadn't realized before that time there were people in the world who didn't have easy access to the Bible in their own language.

Of course, I was in Alaska for another purpose. I was a soldier. My time in the tower became routine. Three and a half years passed quickly, and my reenlistment time came around. What was I going to do? I had joined the U.S. Air Force four years earlier. At that time it was easy for me to think of the world in terms of America versus her enemies. With my conversion to Christ, however, my viewpoint changed. I began to think about the world in terms of God and His enemies, the same ones he was reconciling to Himself through the proclamation of the death and resurrection of his Son (2 Cor. 5:17-21). So I had a choice to make.

After consulting with both my pastor and Craig, I decided not to reenlist. Both of them told me they believed I had the gift of evangelism. They encouraged me to apply to a Bible college and get further training for the ministry. I took their advice and was accepted to attend Moody Bible Institute in downtown Chicago.

PRACTICAL SUGGESTIONS

Let me discuss several things my testimony brings to mind by way of encouragement to young people.

First, over the years I've had the chance to hear the testimonies of many missionary friends. Most never received an extra-biblical call to missions like the prophets and apostles received to do their jobs. By "extra-biblical" I mean supernatural dreams and visions like the apostle Paul saw when a Macedonian man called for help (Acts 16:9). Instead, their stories were always similar in some respects to mine.

My desire for missions grew out of my salvation experience. God had saved me, and as I read the Bible it changed my life. I wanted others to experience that new life too. In obedience both to the clear commands of Scripture, which tell us God is on mission in the world, and the compulsion I felt from the Spirit in my heart, I got involved in a variety of outreaches through both the Church and parachurch organizations.

If you are a young person who thinks he or she might be interested in becoming a fulltime Christian missionary, take a moment to consider whether or not you are currently bearing fruit where God has you. Are you involved in your church? Are you exercising your spiritual gifts, reaching out to people in your community in Jesus' name? If you are not, there is little reason to believe you will go to the other side of the world and do something you aren't doing while at home.

Second, pursuing Christian service was something others encouraged me to do. My pastor recognized the Lord's gifts in my life. My mentor at the servicemen's center saw them as well. So it wasn't merely the testimony of my own heart that compelled me, but there were several witnesses. This gave strength to the conviction I felt, making me feel more confident that it was from the Lord. If you are praying about taking the step toward fulltime Christian service, ask the godly people in your life what they think.

Third, making the decision to pursue fulltime Christian missions was a choice God gave me in his good providence at just the right time. I was unmarried. I had no mortgage, no car payments, no nothing, really. It was just me, an enlistment completely fulfilled, and a future that seemed to say, "God, I'll go wherever and do whatever."

I've known several people over the last decade who decided to enter into fulltime Christian missionary service when they were much older. Some of them had teenage kids. They had already spent many years investing money in purchasing a home or land. Entering fulltime service at that stage in life is possible. This said, I've observed that the young people who made the decision for career missions early seem to have an easier time of it. What is my point? If you are a college-age person and you are bearing fruit where you are and feel compelled toward fulltime foreign missions, now is the time to take that step. It will become more difficult and cumbersome for you if you delay.

CHAPTER TWO

PREPARATION AT MOODY BIBLE INSTITUTE

I had gone through an inductive Bible study on the book of Hebrews during my last year in Alaska. I had also read many books of a more dispensational persuasion. They spoke a great deal about the distinction between ethnic Israel and the Church. Because of this, not to mention the fact our Lord was Jewish according to the flesh, a certain affection for the Jewish people had been cultivated in me, inspiring me to register at Moody in the fall of 1994 under the Jewish studies major. I imagined myself working with Jewish people. I wanted to help them recognize Jesus as their Messiah.

On the strength of my previous references from pastors and friends, the Practical Christian Ministry Department assigned me the ministry of confrontational evangelism for my first year. This meant every Wednesday afternoon when my classes were finished, I went with several other students and started cold-turkey conversations with people, endeavoring to share Christ with those who didn't know him personally. Our efforts at soul winning took us all over the city. We witnessed in the subways, at the local YMCA, and on busy street corners.

Moody Bible Institute is located in the middle of downtown Chicago. Living there was a shock after four years in Alaska. Traffic filled the streets day and night outside my dorm room. Car alarms, police sirens, and the loud, angry voices of annoyed pedestrians filled the air. It was a constant cacophony of noise so strange to me after four years of long, quiet walks in the forest around the military base where I had learned to pray while memorizing and meditating on the Scriptures.

On one occasion during my first year at Moody the hustle and bustle of the city bothered me so much that I packed my bags and got ready to leave for good. I pictured myself backpacking across America or shouldering a giant, wooden cross as I walked through a foreign land like some Christians I had read about. Thankfully the student body president who lived on my floor came into my room as I was about to leave. Seeing my empty shelves and packed bag, he sat down with me and we talked about the anxiety I felt. He prayed with me, and I decided to stick it out.

During my second year I began a series of required systematic theology classes. My professor, Dr. Mayer, was a very devout and serious man who never spoke without thought. Every time the class met he would call the students to attention before bowing his head for prayer. Several moments would pass until all was silent, and just when you expected Dr. Mayer to spout off a mechanical, Lord-thank-you-for-this-day sort of prayer, the silence would continue still one more moment, helping everyone in the room reverently recall that we were addressing the God of the universe. Then he would pray. They were such wonderful prayers. They were never the same, always expressing the deep, meaningful, God-centered theology he was dedicated to teaching.

My practical Christian ministry was changed for my second year. I left confrontational evangelism for street preaching. It was still once a week and entailed going with a group of students to State Street or Michigan Avenue while the crowds were walking back and forth during afternoon rush hour. We would set up an easel and proclaim loudly the message about Jesus. We used various pictures and acrostics painted on paper. These helped carry the message along and hold people's attention. I found this latter form of evangelism less threating to people. They often stood around to listen, and many seeds were planted.

During my sophomore year I got a good job washing windows in the city. I worked for the godly brother of the man who had been my superior in the control tower while in Alaska. I was able to arrange my class schedule so I had a solid two days of washing every week. It didn't matter the season. Winter, spring, summer, and fall, I enjoyed working outdoors with my hands while meeting tons of people from different backgrounds and religions.

One of the managers in a store I washed weekly was an older Jewish woman. We became friends, and she invited me over to her house for a Sabbath meal. I agreed and showed up the following Friday evening. The house was packed. Her husband was there, a well-dressed, high-powered looking man. Extended family and friends were there, too, both men and women most of them considerably older than I was. They walked me through a short ritual in which they lit a golden menorah and sung a song to welcome the Sabbath. Then we all sat down for a large chicken dinner with lots of kosher side dishes.

The food was excellent. I was sitting quietly just listening to the conversation when the store manager who had invited me tapped her wine glass with a spoon. When all was quiet, she drew her guest's attention to me and said, "I've invited Erik over here tonight because I want to understand why he is interested in Jewish studies."

I was indeed in the Jewish studies program at Moody, but up until that point I hadn't taken the first class in the major, a class outlining the long history of the Jews. How helpful that information would have been at that moment! I answered my friend's question and spoke about "Jesus your Messiah."

Looking back I'm able to recognize both the innocence and ignorance of the explanation I gave that evening. It was innocent because Jesus had indeed changed my life by his grace, and I communicated that. I acted in ignorance because had I been more familiar with Jewish history I would have known that just mentioning Jesus' name conjures up a lot of horrible events for many Jewish people. So in retrospect I would have tried to understand their beliefs and assumptions about Jesus before I answered.

After I spoke, several of the women scolded the hostess by asking, "Why did you invite this young man here?" They whispered their disapproval while mentioning Jesus' name in the same sentence with past pogroms and the perpetrators of the Holocaust. One of the men told me his last name was Cohen, reminding me he was from the priestly line. The man of the house was an avid supporter of Jews for Judaism. He attempted to assuage his guests by demanding Jesus couldn't have been the Messiah because he had come from the line of Jehoiachin, a man God had promised would never have another descendent upon the throne (Jer. 22:28-30).[1]

---

[1] Jesus Christ was a long range successor of Jehoiachin, but he wasn't an actual son. He was a *legal* son on account of Joseph being his legal

My relationship with that group of unbelieving Jewish people continued for another semester. The husband welcomed me to their synagogue while I worked on an assignment for my cultural anthropology class. I'll never forget the last conversation I had with him. "My God is a God of justice," he said, pointing to his chest. "But your God," he continued, pointing at me, "is a God of love!" I tried to help him appreciate the idea that in the death of Jesus both the justice and the love of God were expressed, but my words were in vain. He wouldn't listen.

With that conversation, and in light of the more complete understanding of Jewish history I would gain later in the aforementioned class, I began to entertain the idea that perhaps there was another way I might help the Jewish people. I believed God would save the whole nation, but that wouldn't happen until the full number of the Gentiles had come in (Rom. 11:25-32). I began to pray to the Lord, asking Him if it might be better for me to begin thinking about working with unreached Gentiles in the future while never forgetting to pray for the salvation of the remnant of Israel chosen at the present time according to God's grace (Rom. 11:5).

Spring break 1996 rolled around, and I decided to go on a short-term mission trip with the Practical Christian Ministry Department. It was planned for Key West, FL. The assignment was beach evangelism. As I contemplated making my first attempt at raising financial support to do gospel work, I thought to myself, *I*

---

father. Jesus was counted as an *actual* descendant of David from his actual mother, Mary (Geisler & Howe, 277). Joseph came from David's line through David's son, Solomon, as detailed in Matthew's genealogy. Mary came from David's line through his son, Nathan, as detailed in Luke's genealogy.

don't think anyone will partner with me to go to the beach! Nonetheless, I went ahead and wrote my Christian buddies from the military, my family members, and old high school friends who had come to Christ. None of them balked about the balmy location. Indeed, some of them not only gave toward what ended up being a fruitful trip in Florida that year, but they would generously continue their investment toward the work of Christ in and through me (and my family) for years to come.

Now let me get back to academics. When I was young, I hadn't excelled at foreign languages. By the time I had finished all the required classes, I could count to five in German and Spanish. That was it. Therefore, as I thought about taking Greek or Hebrew at Moody, I felt a little intimidated. Instead of trying it, I decided to take some linguistics classes that could be substituted for the language requirement. The first class was called *Introduction to Language.* The second was *Phonetics.* These classes helped prepare me for my summer internship that came between my sophomore and junior years.

The summer internship was a requirement for all students pursuing a degree in missions. While I could've gone anywhere in the world, I recalled the video I had seen while at the servicemen's center in Alaska, the one produced by New Tribes Mission (NTM). With a little research, I discovered NTM had a six-week school designed for such internships. It was located in the mountains near Goroka, Papua New Guinea (PNG). I decided to go and again both sought and received help from those who had supported me in the work of evangelism that spring while I was in Key West.

The NTM program was called Interface. When I arrived, I

soon discovered it wasn't going to be a lazy six weeks. The schedule was filled with meaningful activities. We were taught the Bible chronologically during morning devotions. During the day we had sessions on *Tok Pisin,* the language-of-wider-communication used in PNG. We also studied various worldview topics, addressing them from the Bible. We hiked, explored culture, and prepared for a lengthy village visit during the last weeks of the program.

My summer internship that year was a major turning point in my life. While I was there several things happened. First, I observed a very modest missionary couple living and working in a community in PNG. They had labored at both church planting and translation in that place for many years and were preparing to retire. Being very impressionable at that point about what I might or might not want to do in the future, something really troubled me. After those many years of sacrifice and service, the translation of the New Testament wasn't finished. The dual focus of both church planting and translation had been too large for this one couple.

After the village visit I was seeking the Lord one night outside the dining hall on the Interface campus, prayerfully contemplating a single question. If I had a choice between (a) planting a church, or (b) leaving God's word at the end of many years overseas, which would I choose? I would want to do the latter. That was when it happened. While I sat under the stars shining brightly above, my future suddenly came into clear focus for me. My thoughts had already begun to move toward working with unreached Gentiles. Now I foresaw how I would try to reach them by God's grace. It would be through Bible translation. (Ultimately I ended up in the linguistics major at Moody. I went on to take the challenge of the New Testament Greek courses and found my fear of the classes had been unwarranted.)

The second thing that happened during my summer internship would change my life just as much and more than the choice I was making to move in the direction of Bible translation. I had met a Moody student named Michele Carrow earlier that year. She had just returned from her internship in China shortly before I left for mine. While in PNG I wrote her father and mother a letter and asked them if they would allow me to court their daughter.

Michele had grown up in a solid, mission-minded home, attending both a Christian Missionary Alliance church and a Southern Baptist church. She had been everything I hadn't been as a child. She got excellent grades in school, had a desire for missions since age five, took short-term mission trips to Mexico, Dominica, and inner-city St. Louis during high school. She taught VBS and Sunday school, and attended Flint River Baptist Camp every summer. Teens in the local detention center knew her from weekly visits. When she was sixteen, a friend from church asked her father if he could date and kiss her. Her dad said no. She was too young to date, and kissing was something they expected her to save for the man she would marry.

When her parents got my letter, her father replied and said the decision to date me was up to her. When I received the correspondence after returning from PNG, I went to see her where she worked on campus. I told her about the letter I had written. She was shy and embarrassed about it, but she was pleased, too, and agreed to begin spending more time with me.

Michele and I had already been eating meals together

because she was on my sister floor on campus. Once the relationship was official, however, she began going with me once a week to do open-air evangelism. We attended church together on Sundays. I followed her on her practical Christian ministry and tried to help Spanish speakers learn English. We began reading missionary biographies together in our spare time.

Six months after we had begun dating, while we were playing games at her pastor's home in Chicago, I asked Michele to marry me. She joyfully accepted my proposal. We shared the news with extended family and planned a wedding date for the summer after graduation, a year and a half away! This plan lasted about three months. My window washing job paid good money, and I was having a horrible time keeping my hands off her. So after proving to her father that I could get an apartment and pay the rent for a couple months, her parents agreed to a shorter engagement. We married in Griffin, GA, in Michele's home church between our junior and senior years.

Our last year at Moody Bible Institute was more of the same. We continued in our practical Christian ministries and classes. We worked during our off hours. We cultivated friendships and made sure we were active in the church that would eventually commission us and send us into fulltime Christian missionary service.

Our firstborn son, JohnMark, was born two weeks before graduation. Within two months we had taken him across the country to Idlewild, CA, where we attended Wycliffe Bible Translator's candidate school. We were accepted as members. The following fall we moved to Dallas, TX, where we began graduate work at the Graduate Institute of Applied Linguistics (GIAL). I focused on Bible translation, Michele on literacy. We were there two and a half years. I continued washing windows. Michele gave birth to our daughter, Sierra, and our second son, David. We traveled often, speaking in churches and spreading a vision for Bible translation, asking others to partner with us in the work. By the middle of 2001 the Lord had prepared us and raised up a team to stand behind us. We were ready for the field. There was only one problem. We weren't sure where to go!

PRACTICAL SUGGESTIONS

One of the things four years in Bible school and an additional two-plus years in graduate school required was patience, and not everyone I knew exercised it. A girl I had become acquainted with was intent on getting to the mission field fast. She left Moody for another school that had a shorter academic program. She never finished, and sadly she never ended up on the mission field. Another buddy was swimming in debt from poor financial choices he had made and as a result had to leave. Others had different reasons for not sticking it out until the end.

If you are a young person eager to get to the field, patience is going to be important for you. The wonderful thing about Moody Bible Institute and many other Christian colleges and seminaries is the students who attend them are required to participate in practical Christian ministries outside of class. All the evangelism I engaged in over those years helped me continue bearing fruit in Christ while applying what I was being taught in the classroom. I didn't apply those lessons only then. Over the years I've relied again and again upon the insights given to me in classes like those taught by Dr. Mayer.

When I was at Moody during my first two years, I met several young women. They all loved the Lord, and many of them became my friends. With some I ran for exercise. With others I enjoyed a cup of coffee or an evening walk to a practical Christian ministry that requiring a male chaperone. One young lady really enjoyed playing piano. Sometimes I sang hymns with her as she practiced. It was a joyful and innocent time. It was a time when pursuing someone with the intentions of marriage was a real possibility.

In my case I never felt liberty in my conscience to pursue any of my female friends. It wasn't until I met Michele and had gone to PNG that I was released to do that. Why? I'm sure it was on account of the focus of our lives. Michele had always wanted to be a missionary. She would obey the Great Commission whether I had come into her life or not. Once the direction of my life was confirmed in my heart, I felt free to pursue her. Then we could go together.

I risk stating the obvious on this point, especially since I know the Lord is already leading and teaching you if you are a young person pursuing missions. Yet I might as well say it. You don't want to end up overseas with a spouse who feels they were brought against their will. So before you tie the knot, perhaps you should prayerfully evaluate your motives. Is it simply attraction? Is it only because he or she is a nice Christian man or woman? If you are pursuing missions, it ought to be both of those things plus a settled conviction that you are both headed in the same direction independent of one another.

Finally, just a note on support raising or "partnership development" as it's called these days. I consider this a blessing. While I've had to start many cold-turkey conversations about Christ over the years, I've never had to make a cold-turkey contact with a church, asking them to allow me to come and speak with their congregation. Beginning with that first trip to Key West, FL, and later the trip to PNG, and now on this long term endeavor in the South Pacific, the Lord has always met our financial and prayer needs using family, friends, and various churches who have had a relationship with us.

    The Christian missionary cannot accomplish anything on his own. He needs a loving network of dedicated Christian men, women, and churches committed to the cause he is engaged in. Work on your relationships with those people and churches now. Be involved in their lives and ministries. If you do that, there's a good chance when the time comes for you to "Go!" they will enthusiastically jump behind you and graciously become the agents sending you on your way.

CHAPTER THREE

MY FIRST YEAR OVERSEAS - HEARTSICK

How did you end up in Southeast Tanna, Vanuatu? I've been asked that question many times, and there are more ways than one to answer it. I could focus on the human element, explaining how I first got exposed to Vanuatu, how I researched it and then got assigned there by a committee. I could also focus on the divine element, quoting Bible verses: "To man belong the plans of the heart, but from the Lord comes the reply of the tongue" (Prov. 16:9). "Heaven rules" (Dan. 4:26). Both the human and the divine elements were essential components in the process, and both are true.

Let me start with the human element. When Michele and I got to Dallas in the fall of 1998 to begin graduate work, we didn't know where we were going to serve. As I mentioned before, Michele had been on several mission trips when she was young to the island of Dominica, and then she went to China while attending Moody. I had been only to PNG. Unreached non-Jewish groups were still very much in my heart, and on the ground I had three babies in diapers. Where would my family fit with that mix?

We began talking to staff members at GIAL who had served in various parts of the world. We listened to their stories and attended chapel services where furloughing missionaries would speak. We heard about Europe and Asia, West and Central Africa, Indonesia, Mexico and South America, and many other places located in what came to be known as "The Wide World of Wycliffe." We spent time in the partnership development office looking over detailed reports on specific people groups. The reality was there were needs everywhere, and while we spent countless hours praying about it and talking, we just didn't know how to choose.

Some relief came during a sociolinguistics class I had been taking. An enthusiastic proponent of Bible translation detailed the sociolinguistic challenges in the Solomon Islands where he and his family had worked for a decade, finishing a complete translation of the Bible with the help of skilled partners. (Solomon Islands is in the South Pacific. American soldiers fought there at Guadalcanal during World War II.) After that class, Michele and I began researching that region of the world.

Things being what they were back then the decision ultimately rested with an independent group of seasoned Wycliffe missionaries. The assignment committee met in 1999 and prayerfully considered the short sheet of paper we had filled out indicating our preferences. It said we were very open to serving anywhere in the world. Unreached with no church wasn't our primary priority. We were willing to go where missionaries had gone before so long as the need for translation had been identified. We would prefer homeschooling over boarding school, though we weren't completely opposed to the latter. While we were open to anywhere, we had begun researching several places. If they considered them, would they please allow the following priority: (1) the Solomon Islands, (2) Vanuatu, and (3) PNG. After deliberation they finally put an end to the mystery. The Solomon Islands had had recent political turmoil, but Vanuatu had invited us. We were asked whether or not we would accept.

Michele and I did accept the invitation and promptly got in contact with the leadership in the Vanuatu Branch. We asked them if they knew ahead of time the specific people we would be serving. They informed us their intention was to send us to a language community on the largest island in the archipelago, Espiritu Santo. We were overjoyed at this clear direction and communicated our enthusiasm to the churches and friends who had already become our financial and prayer partners.

What exactly did we communicate to them at the time? We told them the obvious facts about Vanuatu, the ones we had learned from research. Population about 220,000. More languages per capita than any other country in the world. English and French were the languages for education. *Bislama,* an English-based pidgin, was the national language. Animism was the traditional religion. A rich Christian heritage had turned the people from cannibalism and tribal fighting. London Missionary Society had come first in 1839, then the Presbyterians and Anglicans, followed by both the Catholics and Seventh Day Adventists, and finally various Pentecostal groups. A complete Bible in *Bisluma* had been published by the United Bible Society in the late 1990s.

We also communicated with conviction the information we had been told by other missionaries who had answered our questions when we had inquired more carefully about the exact need for missionary work, specifically Bible translation. We said things like the complete Bible in the language of wider communication wasn't understood by people. The people in the churches were "skin-Christians," just going through the motions of worship while still being animists in their hearts. Bible translation was a necessary exercise to help bring clarity and dispel the harmful confusion.

We left America in the fall of 2001 and went to Wycliffe's Pacific Orientation Course in PNG. We spent 4 months there learning as much as we could about Melanesian culture and history. They taught us *Tok Pisin,* which I had begun learning back in 1996 during my summer internship. The last part of the course was a six-week village stay on a small island off the coast.

During our six-week village stay we were adopted into a PNG family. They opened their home to us and introduced us to a number of new things. We learned to plant yams in a garden, how to spear fish, and how to balance in a "bush toilet" constructed on a cliff dangling out over the rolling surf. We slept in a thatch house built on posts. All five of us were in one room and learned to fall asleep listening to large, grunting pigs as they rolled around in the ground outside directly underneath us. The whole course was a stretching, eye-opening experience.

The day finally arrived when we flew to Port Vila, the capital city of Vanuatu located on Efate Island. Its population was about 40,000 at that time. Situated right on the ocean, the air was salty and humid. The beautiful aqua-blue waters in the bay and a large tourist ship that arrived every couple weeks made us feel we had arrived in the Bahamas. A single, one-way road ran along the coast through the middle of downtown. You could get from one side to the other in less than two minutes when the traffic wasn't at a standstill on account of hundreds of box-like cars used as taxis.

We jumped right into adjusting. Within four weeks our shipment of six crates and a couple barrels arrived from the United States. We began making the switch from *Tok Pisin* to *Bislama*. We made contact with one of the elders in the village we would be living in on Espiritu Santo. He joyfully informed us an old missionary house had been fixed up for our family. We were welcomed and told to come any time.

We left Efate Island and made our way to what we thought would be our new long-term home. The house the people had thoughtfully cleaned up for us was better than anything they had in their village. It had been constructed by missionaries from a previous generation. The walls were hard timber. The corrugated iron on the roof had rusted, but it didn't leak. To our surprise, it even had a toilet inside, and a bathtub! It was situated next to a large, cement-brick Presbyterian church. From the front door we could look down and see the whole village of just under 1,000 people.

We quickly learned the rich history of the place. When the early missionaries had arrived in the mid 1800s, they established that village as a safe haven. People from warring tribes could flee there and live while being taught the message about Jesus Christ. It was the largest rural village on the coast. An English-based, government-run high school was on the hill just a stone's throw from our house and attracted kids from all over the island. A beautiful, white-sand beach was a five minute walk away. A couple times a month a cruise ship would come and drop a thousand tourists off to spend the day there.

When we settled in to start our work, we were in for a bit of a shock. We expected to hear the vernacular (the local language of the people) spoken all the time. The opposite was true. Inside homes many men had married women from other languages. Out of necessity the parents spoke to one another and their children in *Bislama*. When we went to church, the people used *Bislama*. When there were community meetings, it was largely the same. I often made my way over to the high school where the kids spoke to one another in *Bislama*. When they saw me, they liked trying to speak English with a native speaker.

Since the vernacular wasn't spoken much, at least not in the open, I used to take a small hand-held recorder into the village and ask people to tell me stories, which I would later transcribe. I had been working hard at it for some time, always a little perplexed in the back of my mind about why exactly I had been sent to that location despite all the sociolinguistic factors making vernacular translation appear to be an unnecessary exercise. It took about eight months when something happened to clarify things for me.

One afternoon, having decided to get some stories, I went to see an influential old man who had been well educated. He was sitting outside his thatch house throwing coconut grounds to some chickens and cats gathered around his bare feet. His clothes were tattered and his eyes tired. When he finished with the animals, I handed him my audio recorder and asked him to tell me a story.

"What would you like me to tell you?" he asked.

"Anything is fine, sir," I said.

He thought about it before nodding his head slowly. He began, "Several years ago, the Presbytery met. We were talking about how respect has deteriorated in our community. The children no longer listen to the chiefs, and they drink too much *kava* and alcohol. We decided to ask the translation people in Vila to send someone who will help us restore our language and teach the young people respect. That was several years ago, and now you have come."

It was an honest confession that broke my heart. I hurt for this man and his generation living at a time of tremendous upheaval. With the large town of Luganville only a forty-five minute drive down the coastal road, the modern world had forced its way in and had set their once isolated, quiet culture on the fast track of change. The presence of a strong language-of-wider-communication, intermarriage, a multi-language schooling policy, an influx of tourists together with foreign videos and media, it had all worked together to erode both the vernacular language and the cultural moorings of this Melanesian community.

That conversation confirmed for me what I had been fearing for some time. The people wanted us to save their language! I didn't consider that part of my job description. I had trained and come overseas to help facilitate translation in a place where people needed it in order to understand the Bible. I wasn't interested in preserving language. I respectfully informed our field leadership. They were disappointed and tried to persuade us otherwise, but I was adamant. As a result, they offered me an office job back in the capital city. It would hold Michele and me until we could recover from our disappointment and prayerfully consider what to do next.

The Bible says, "Hope deferred makes the heart sick . . ." (Prov. 13:12). That is exactly how I felt at that point in my life. My whole first year overseas seemed to me nothing more than one long, expensive waste of time. I didn't know how to recover, either. Questions plagued me on my bed at night and seemed to paralyze me: *Did I spend many years training to do something unnecessary? Maybe I should look into other countries where the people are more unreached and the need for translation more apparent? Would it be fair to our supporters if we do that? Will we have to go through another orientation course? What about my three babies? What if we go somewhere else and it all falls apart?*

My disappointment lasted several months, but light came when a new translation team arrived and got assigned to Tanna. They had been there several months when they invited me to come down and help them build their village home. I went and was pleasantly surprised to see that life in their rural community was much different than what I had experienced previously in the larger village near a large town. The people spoke their vernacular language all the time, and the spiritual struggle they were having to understand the Bible was much more apparent.

I returned to Port Vila and was working in the office when a Tannese pastor came and sought me out. He informed me the people in Southeast Tanna needed a translation. They had a New Testament earlier missionaries had done in the late 1800s, but it wasn't used or understood anymore. I was suspicious, but I went ahead and asked my boss his thoughts. He didn't want my family to quit missions, and he didn't relish the idea of us going to another field. Therefore, he allowed me to do whatever it took to be convinced of the need.

I returned to Tanna at a later date and backpacked around the whole language community in Southeast Tanna. I went from village to village, asking questions about intermarriage rates and language use. I tested the old translation for comprehension. The tests showed men tended to marry within the language community.

Vernacular was being used in the churches and homes. There were few extant copies of the old translation, and the language had changed considerably. Comfortable with the long term viability of the language and the need for translation, I agreed to the pastor's request and decided to move my family to Tanna in the fall of 2003.

I suggested previously that there was both a human element in our plans *and* a divine element. Let me focus on the latter. Why did God in His good providence ordain that I go through all that training and partnership development and travel to the ends of the earth only to end up spending a year in a place where the need for Bible translation wasn't obvious? In retrospect I've been able to recognize at least two reasons.

First and the most obvious, my going to that community with my family was a wonderful, albeit belated and expensive way to perform a sociolinguistic survey. The world is full of languages and people groups. In order for us (I mean the Church universal on mission to reach the nations) to get an accurate, up-to-date assessment of their gospel-centered needs, someone needs to go there with gospel-centered glasses and check things out. My family and I did that for a year, and in the future, if someone wants to go to that community and labor in Christ's name, the information we gathered (especially for someone wanting to do translation) might prove helpful before they make a commitment.

I like to think God ordained that year of my life for a second reason as well, namely, so I could share my experiences with you and give you something to think about before you go overseas. With that in mind let me share some practical suggestions.

PRACTICAL SUGGESTIONS

Many fulltime Christian missionaries who go overseas never make it past their first term. I have seen evidence that this is indeed the case. I nearly quit during my first year. I've also watched many good-intentioned friends crash and burn shortly after their arrival. The truth of the matter is that the "successful" long-term missionary is the exception rather than the rule. Why? There are just so many things to shake one's faith, causing discouragement and intimidation. Plain old culture shock is enough, but add to the mix things like doctrinal and cultural differences between colleagues when different denominations and nationalities are involved, community expectations, immorality, isolation, financial matters, physical health, inability to learn the local language, etc., and this is just the beginning of the challenges.

In my case it wasn't any of those things that nearly did me in. It was unspoken expectations and the sickness of heart that came from not having those expectations fulfilled. For years I had imagined I would be working with an unreached people group. I hid that strong desire when the assignment committee met. I told them it really didn't matter if the people were reached or not as long as there was a need for translation. I ended up in a place where the gospel was widespread, but I had been comforted by the assessment of others who had said the people were only Christians on the surface and needed vernacular translation to understand the Bible. In the end, however, it was all about language preservation in the minds of the people we went to serve. I became despondent.

If you would like to avoid such heart-sickness, I would suggest the following remedies:

First, you need to pay special attention to the unspoken expectations you have before going overseas. For example, if you strongly imagine the Lord wants you to work with people who are unreached in the traditional 10/40-Window sense of the word, you need to make that clear in your preferences when the place of service is being chosen by or for you. If you are not going to act on that impulse toward unreached people and accept the assignment to a place where the gospel is widespread, you need to consciously release the former expectation to the Lord and no longer hang onto it. If you hang onto it, it will cause you to stumble indefinitely.

Second, unless you intend to go overseas and simply do whatever seems good, you need to get a clear understanding of both the spiritual need(s) where you are going and the role you will fill to help meet it. Simply saying things like "I'm going to go preach the gospel," or "I'm going to go make disciples of all the nations," that isn't enough. It behooves you to find out the who, what, when, where, why, and how of the job. Get all the details that will help you gain understanding. The picture of the ministry you will be involved in must be based on factual information, and it needs to be accurately and honestly presented to your supporters.

The easiest way to get that sort of information is by going to the field of service before you actually make a long-term commitment. Short-term missions can be a very helpful way to accomplish this.

In some cases it might not be possible to go first and check out the place where you are prayerfully thinking about serving. If you are unable to go first, you will be depending on the perceptions of others. In such a case you should ask all the aforementioned questions. Don't be afraid to get clarification. The missionaries already on the field in all probability will be happy to answer your questions. It's likely the excitement they will feel over the possibility of you coming to join their team will equal or even exceed the excitement you feel over the possibility of going to join it.

Whether you go ahead of time or go depending upon the perceptions of other, you need to be ready to adjust your expectations as necessary. That's just another way of saying you need to be flexible. If you are flexible like a young tree branch (to use a simile common in these parts), you can be bent as outward forces dictate, grow, and go on to bear fruit. If you are inflexible, however, like a full grown tree branch, the pressure of change might break you and destroy your ability to bear fruit in the long run.

I nearly broke during that first year, but I'm thankful to God that he gave me enough flexibility to consider another assignment in Vanuatu. Had I left disappointed after that first year, I wouldn't have gone on to discover the great satisfaction felt in seeing men and women, both reached and unreached, experience hearing God's oracles expressed in their heart language.

CHAPTER FOUR

INTRODUCTION TO TANNA

The town of Lenakel is located on the western side of Tanna Island. It's a small town with only a handful of stores lining the dusty street. Some are made of woven bamboo and coconut thatch. Others are constructed with sheets of corrugated roofing iron nailed hastily to wooden frames. Local residents who have done well have made their stores with cement bricks. No matter the construction materials, all the stores sell the same basic wares, including canned fish, flour, rice, cooking oil, sugar, and a variety of cheap knick-knacks.

While Lenakel is small, it's definitely not scorned. The short, fierce-faced Melanesians on Tanna are fond of calling it "Blackman Town." The title is a boast, really, the people's way of saying all the shops are proudly owned and operated by locals. This is in contrast to the larger towns in the northern part of the archipelago, Port Vila on Efate Island and Luganville on Espiritu Santo, both of which have large numbers of Asian shop owners.

Monday and Friday are market days in Lenakel. Folks from miles around venture out early and make the trek. Those with extra cash on hand will jump on one of the local four-wheel-drive trucks. Those wanting to save money will walk. When they arrive in town the place is bustling with people comparing prices in the stores. Long lines await those coming on Friday to the bank, a small room located in the middle of town. Those in search of meat will visit one of several bamboo huts where fresh cow carcasses are hung from the rafters on large hooks. The market is always full. Depending on the season there are yams, manioc, taro, sweet potatoes, cabbage, onions, carrots, *kava,* watermelons, bananas, passion fruit, coconuts, lemons, oranges, papaya, dried tobacco, and assorted other crops for sale.

The majority of people living on Tanna are subsistence farmers. When faced with the large economic gap that exists between the majority of the population and Westerners, it's not uncommon to hear people clicking tongue-and-cheek, saying, "Money is the foreigner's garden!"

It's true. The Tannese recognize money makes the foreigners' world go around, but they also recognize that tourists treasure books. They observe them reading at the airport and at several resorts and bungalows frequented by those wanting to see *Yasur*, a spectacular, active volcano located on the eastern side of the island.

It wouldn't be fair to suggest no one on Tanna reads. Some do. It's simply that very few read in their own vernacular. The numbers are quite astounding. On Tanna alone, an island with only about 30,000 people, seven languages are spoken.

This diversity makes education a challenge. Which language should the schools use? The official policy states that preschool, kindergarten, and first grade are to be taught at the village level in the vernacular. Such a goal is lofty indeed, requiring at least a handful of people in each area to possess skills in orthography development and dictionary making. A wealth of books in the vernacular are necessary as well. While the Department of Education has run many workshops in partnership with the Summer Institute of Linguistics over the years in an effort to teach all these skills, in most areas a robust vernacular program for the early grades remains an unrealized ideal.

When the children transition into second grade, they are thrown into the strange world of either English or French. This scheme was a natural outgrowth of the nation's independence, which was won in 1980 from the colonial powers who had governed them. Few of the students, especially in rural areas, achieve more than a basic understanding and are forced to leave school after eighth grade. Those who go on, even if they learn the language reasonably well, have few opportunities to use it outside of the class-room. Instead, they return to their villages where life is a daily grind of gardening and resolving community conflicts. English or French become something of the past.

The traditional religion on Tanna is animism. Most people believe they have lived on Tanna since the beginning of time. Their ancestors were born from stones, each of them associated with some essential element in their daily lives. For example, in all the villages, one or more families will claim to have come from the yam stone, one or more from this or that fish stone, and still others from the taro stone and so forth. As a result, each family has a certain status in the community. They are recognized as the power brokers responsible to care for their ancestral stone. By doing this they ensure such things as good crops, successful fishing ventures, or the healing of this or that ailment.

It's impossible to talk about Tanna without addressing *kava*.

The consumption of this sedative tree root is one method the Tannese use to divide their day. In the area where we work, it is common for the people to divide the day between the morning *(ia napnapen)*, midday *(ia rukwasikar)*, afternoon *(ia naruarav)*, and finally the time for *kava* *(napen savei nekava)*. The later part of the day begins in the late afternoon between four and five, just about the time the cicadas begin to chirp loudly.

When the time for *kava* arrives, the men from the village go and meet in a place called the *nakamal,* which is situated under large *nabanga* trees. (While women are allowed in the *nakamal* during court cases during the day, it's strictly forbidden for women to come to the *nakamal* during this time.) The men come carrying branches of the *kava* plant. They sit down together around a fire and chat while using abrasive coconut fibers or small knives to meticulously clean the dirt from the *kava* root. If there are bad spots on the plant, they will carefully cut them out. After the root is cleaned, they chew it with HUGE mouthfuls. They spit it out on leaves, put it into another more porous fiber found on the coconut tree, pour water over it, wring it out into dried coconut shells, and then drink the contents down with a loud spitting sound when finished.

After a person drinks the shell of *kava,* he spits out the dregs. Often times he will speak either a curse or a blessing. This practice is called *tamafa.* The frequency of taking *tamafa* is up to the person performing it. This said, there are certain times when it's expected to be performed in order to invoke a blessing — e.g. when a newborn child's umbilical cord falls off and they have their first bath, when a young boy is circumcised, when a girl starts her period, when a young man shaves for the first time, and when people are sick and it's prescribed as part of a remedy.

When the gospel first came to Tanna, the early missionaries weren't welcomed. The first was John Williams, a missionary with the London Missionary Society who worked in Samoa. He came ashore in Port Resolution 1839. He left three Samoans to check out the place and preceded to Erromango, the island just north of Tanna. When he and his young missionary companion Harris arrived there, the inhabitants promptly clubbed them to death on the beach and then ate them (Paton, 75).

Several other European missionaries followed. Dr. Turner and Henry Nisbet with their wives settled in Port Resolution in 1842. They were there seven months before being driven away with the Samoan missionaries by the angry Tannese (Miller Bk. I, 35). In the years 1858-1862, three more European missionary couples attempted to settle in Southeast Tanna – the Patons, the Johnstons, and the Mathesons. They, like Dr. Turner with Henry Nisbet and the Samoans before them, were also driven away by hostilities. Finally, in 1869, William Watt and his wife Agnes both arrived in *Kwamera*, a village many miles southwest of Port Resolution. They were welcomed and spent the next thirty years working with the inhabitants in that area of the island (Miller Bk. I, 189).

Presbyterians worked all over Tanna during the latter part of the 1800s and into the early part of the 1900s. They were Sabbatarians and thus had strict rules about what was and wasn't lawful to do on Sunday: no carrying knives, no gardening, no fishing, no cooking. Rules like that were enshrined in their liturgy. The Presbyterian mission stations were responsible for teaching the locals how to read and write. They taught in the local dialects. This continued until the Presbyterian church gained their independence in 1948.

Kava drinking was strictly forbidden by the early missionaries, not only on Sunday but all the time. This continued until 1940 when a mysterious figure arrived on Tanna. He was dressed in white trousers, long sleeve shirt and hat, with a veil obscuring his face. He appeared and spoke in a strange voice. His name was John Frum (Lindstrom 1981, 102). John initially began teaching the people to obey the government and the missionaries. With time, however, the movement he spawned became focused on cultural revitalization. His followers rejected the strict rules of the missionaries, took their kids from school, and returned to their *kava* and their customs.

The John Frum Movement still exists today on Tanna. The largest concentration of followers is on the eastern side of the island near Port Resolution and Sulfur Bay. John Frum's followers meet on Fridays and sing songs unique to their beliefs, beliefs which keep their members hoping that someday John will come back and bring great wealth from America.

In addition to widespread Christianity and the John Frum Movement other religions are active on Tanna. Muslims have recently arrived and are working in the middle of the island. Their evangelistic endeavors began with a family of John Frum followers. They are gaining momentum by offering to pay school fees for anyone willing to send their children away to be instructed in Islamic teaching. The Mormon Church is active on Tanna as well. They offer special incentives to their members much like the Muslims. They pay school fees, give food, and buy water tanks for communities. In addition to the Muslims and the LDS Church, there are Baha'i worshippers on the island and undoubtedly other non-Christian and cult groups I'm unaware of.

PRACTICAL SUGGESTIONS

No matter where you go in the world you can be sure that place has a long history. The more you know about that history the better equipped you will be to understand the current situation on the ground. Most mission agencies would include at least some historical orientation when you first arrive in the county. Yet you will want to do your own research as well before leaving for the field. Your research should consider the nation as a whole and the specific area and people you are prayerfully thinking about serving. Some good research questions that just begin to scratch the surface include the following:

1. How effective are the local Christians in reaching their own community with the gospel?
2. Does this country have a history of being a colony of a Western nation? If so, which one? When did they gain their independence and under what circumstances? What form of government does this nation have today? Is the political system stable or are there frequent upheavals?
3. What is the primary religion of this country? What is the attitude of this country toward Christian missionaries?
4. How many languages are spoken in this country? Is there a national language? Are there "local" languages spoken by different groups? What is the government's official policy regarding the language used for education?
5. Have there been anthropologists or linguists who have done

any research in the specific area where you want to work? (The research of others, even secular anthropologists, can be very helpful for the prospective missionary as they research a people.)
6. Have other missionaries worked in the area before? If so, who were they and what denomination(s) were they affiliated with? What sort of work did they accomplish? Translation work? Church planting?
7. What kind of non-Christian missionary activity has gone on in this area? Are there cults and cargo-cults present? What are their beliefs? Are they making a significant impact?

PART TWO

Cultures around the world are different. I was taught that axiom during my undergraduate years while sitting through classes on anthropology and missions at Moody Bible Institute. Downtown Chicago was a wonderful place to realize just how true it was. A melting pot of the Midwest, cultural variety was always on display in that teeming metropolis. In one part of town authentic Puerto Rican foods and music greeted the senses. In other parts of town there were Chinese, Korean, Mexican, Italian, Indian, and more cultures on display.

I was taught other helpful axioms as well during my time of preparation. I wish all those axioms were still fresh in my mind, but unfortunately I've forgotten some of them over the years. While that's true, several of the truths have come to mind frequently while living overseas. I'm thankful I was taught them before leaving my home country. The rest of this book is dedicated to those helpful, worthwhile truths I hope will benefit you, the hopeful missionary.

CHAPTER FIVE

AXIOM ONE — MAINTAIN YOUR SPIRITUAL VITALITY

What is spiritual vitality? Spiritual vitality is keeping our relationship with God the Father, the Son, and the Holy Spirit vibrant and strong. It involves keeping our consciences clean and tender by confessing and forsaking known sin. It entails holding onto what we already have from God, living according to it, while purposefully putting ourselves into a position where we will obtain more. This means more knowledge of the Scriptures gained from the Holy Spirit as we meditate on them, memorize them, and listen to them read and preached. It also involves more experiential knowledge of God as we learn to walk with him by faith in new areas of life. As we pray continually to him both alone and corporately, we wait on him to answer. We watch him provide for our needs according to his will. We also delight to see him lift up his reputation through us as we use our spiritual gifts to build up the Body of Christ. Why do Christians need to maintain their spiritual vitality? It's necessary because we are in a spiritual battle. On the outside we struggle against Satan and the worldly system he controls. On the inside we are constantly assaulted by sinful desires that wage war against us (1 Pet. 2:11)

Maintaining our spiritual vitality keeps us strong for the struggle. A popular illustration of this is seen in the gospels. Jesus was led into the desert to be tempted by the Devil. He spent time fasting and praying. His mind was saturated with God's Word. When Satan came to tempt him and twisted the truth, Jesus defeated him by quoting the Scriptures.

It's true that Jesus is the impeccable Son of God. "This means . . . that it was impossible for him to sin" (Berkhof, 318). Yet his method of resisting temptation provides a model for Christians to follow. We need to maintain our communion with Christ who lives within us. We need to fill our minds with the Bible. This leads to overcoming. The apostle John said, "I write to you, young men, because you are strong, and the word of God lives in you, and you have overcome the evil one" (1 John 2:14).

If maintaining our spiritual vitality keeps us strong, the opposite is also true. Failing to maintain it makes us more susceptible to falling into prolonged, willful sin with all its destructive potential. It can ruin our assurance of salvation, our testimony, and the relationships we hold dear. Missionaries aren't immune to this tragic possibility. Let me share several stories of missionaries who have fallen. (Names, places, and specific details have been changed for the sake of those involved.)

EXAMPLE ONE

Ben was from America. He was commissioned by his church and sent to go serve overseas as a Bible translator. He had a devout wife. Together they had three young children, a boy and two girls. It took them several months, but they finally got to their village allocation where they expected to work for the next ten to twelve years.

Ben loved everything about his job. He thrived in the village setting. He found learning the people's language and culture an easy task. He worked at it joyfully day and night. His wife was just the opposite. She didn't enjoy living in the village. Language learning was difficult. Her days were filled from dawn to dusk with caring for all their children's physical and educational needs. She woke up tired and went to bed tired.

Ben and his wife both knew in their minds how important it was to maintain their spiritual vitality as individuals and as a family, yet they didn't make time for devotions and prayer. Ben justified himself. He reasoned he was a Bible translator. He already knew what the Scriptures said. He didn't take the time to lead his family by providing diligent instruction in the things of the Lord.

As time went on Ben and his wife began a slow drift. They drifted from the Lord. They drifted from one another. Fights become more frequent. Discontentment, anger, impatience, and unkind words began to mark their once loving, patient, joyful, Spirit-filled personalities.

Ben's work began to take him to other villages where he would check how well the drafts he and his committee had produced were communicating. On one occasion he met a young national woman who showed him attention. She sat with him and asked questions about his life. When he said something funny, she would reach out and slap his arm playfully.

Before leaving that afternoon Ben broke a cultural taboo. He made prolonged eye contact with this young woman. As he walked home, he began to replay the flirtatious moments he had shared with her in his mind. Having left the Spirit-led discipline of taking his every thought captive to make it obey Christ, he soon found his imagination alive with immoral thoughts.

Satan got a foothold in Ben's unguarded heart. It was easy to do, too, since for a long time Ben hadn't been coming to the Lord daily, confessing his sins and seeking to keep his relationship with the Lord fresh. Instead, he had been relying on past grace which in this case couldn't pull him from the edge of the pit where he found himself.

Ben began to make excuses to make it back to that village. Within a year he began to have a secret relationship with the young woman. In the end, he had to leave the non-profit organization he had been serving with. He lost his marriage. His children, though they had only felt admiration and affection for their father, began a life-long struggle dealing with disappointment and anger.

EXAMPLE TWO

The year was 1995. Bill and his wife, Dianne, were sent out as missionaries. When they arrived on the field, they settled down to life in a village close to some colleagues they had gone to Bible school with. Once a week they would meet to fellowship while their children played together. Relationships were good. Everything seemed fine.

After a few years Bill and Dianne went on furlough. Bill needed to get some additional training. During the week he attended classes, and then traveled home on weekends to be with his family. While he was at the school, he got involved with pornography. He began frequenting Christian chat rooms on the Internet. It wasn't long before Bill began communicating regularly with a woman he had met online. After a couple months they arranged a meeting, and then spent the night in a hotel.

Bill's wife, Dianne, discovered some incriminating emails. When she confronted her husband, he assured her that everything was behind them. It was all taken care of. They returned to the field without telling appropriate authorities in their mission organization about Bill's sinful behavior.

While on the field, Dianne found out Bill had been lying. It wasn't over. He was still buying the woman gifts on the Internet. Their friends were home on furlough, but Dianne confided in them by email, telling them about Bill's ongoing infidelity. She plead with them, "Please don't tell anyone. Only God can truly change his heart, not man." Yet how could their friends be silent? The organization they were part of had strict rules about such things. They told Dianne the whole sinful saga needed to be exposed if healing were ever to be possible. If Bill and Dianne didn't confess to the leadership themselves, then in one month's time their friends would be forced to do it.

Leadership was informed. When Bill was reprimanded, he agreed to get some counseling. He and Dianne left the field and returned to their home country. Although they tried to work through their marital problems, Bill had already decided to leave his wife and kids. He wanted to be with the other woman.

When he left them, he took for himself all the money they had saved. He continued looking at pornography. He began smoking and started to drink more heavily.

Well, that was in 1995. Today Bill has repented of his sin and is back in church. Yet the sinful hiatus he took in the pit of willful sin has had tragic results in his life. Like Ben, he lost his marriage. Though he apologized to his children, his relationship with them will never be the same. And what about the work he was sent to accomplish in God's harvest field? It was sacrificed on the altar of sinful desire.

EXAMPLE THREE

Bob and Sue were Christian missionaries. They were young with no children. After they arrived in their country of service, they quickly became a good example to the missionary community. Everyone looked up to them because they came and integrated well with the nationals. They were content to live with less and lodged in a room with a local family. They were very involved with nationals in the community.

After a year or two it was time to sign the doctrinal statement of their mission organization. Bob and Sue had signed years before, but this time they were having problems with it. Sue no longer believed in the inerrancy of Scripture. Maybe most of it was inspired, but it certainly couldn't be every word. She saw contradictions in parallel passages.

The mission organization sent some respected leaders to talk with them. They explained the organization's position on inerrancy. Passages that seemed to have contradictions in them were talked about. Solutions were discussed. It didn't help Sue in her struggle with unbelief. She convinced Bob her views were right, and they continued to refuse the signing of the doctrinal statement.

The two of them went home on a leave of absence from the mission organization. Sue plugged back into her church. Then she began wanting to have an experience with the Holy Spirit. She began fasting. She would eat only at night. She continued for more than forty days while asking God to give her his Holy Spirit in a miraculous way.

God didn't answer Sue in the manner she wanted. As a result her heart became hardened in unbelief. Bob's heart followed hers. The two of them decided to leave the Christian faith. They sent out an email to all their Christian friends. They asked them to stop writing them. They cut ties with the Church.

Consider the first two case studies above. They have one thing in common. The fall of Ben and Bill into adultery began with secret sin. Why did they keep it secret? Because they knew what they were doing was shameful. Causing Christians to willfully participate in this sort of behavior is a favorite weapon of the Devil.

If Satan succeeds in tempting Christians to do shameful things we know are wrong, two things happen. First, our conscience becomes defiled and we no longer have the peace of God. Second, our spiritual lives come to a standstill.

Regarding the second point, consider the sin of Achan after the Israelites conquered Jericho. He took some of the spoils God had told the people not to touch. When the people went to conquer Ai, God didn't go with them. He stopped blessing them with victory against their enemies until the secret things Achan had sinfully hidden in his tent were dealt with (Jos. 7:20).

If we have secret sins in our lives, we need to bring them out into the open and forsake them. If we don't, our unhealthy spiritual condition will fester like a dirty wound, causing our relationship with Christ to suffer. We will become increasingly uncomfortable around our Christian brothers and sisters. We might slide back into the world until there's no noticeable difference between us and unbelievers. When we are living that way, we lose our assurance of salvation. *In Chosen by God,* R.C. Sproul made the following observation:

> The greatest peril to our continued assurance is a fall into some serious and gross sin. We know the love that covers a multitude of sins. We know we don't have to be perfect to have the assurance of salvation. But when we fall into special sorts of sins, our assurance is shaken brutally (172).

Of course, it's possible for Christians who are participating in prolonged secret sins to continue going to church. The danger with such hypocrisy, however, is that we end up like the people of Judah in the years leading up to the Babylonian captivity. They were very religious, giving sacrifices and coming frequently to God's temple. Yet God wasn't pleased with them. He didn't want religious activity. He wanted clean hands and righteous living (Isa. 1:10-17).

It's a bad thing when any Christian willfully participates in secret sin. This is true, and yet there is something worse. It's the Christian missionary participating in such behavior. Just think about it. The Christian missionary is more often than not commissioned by the Church with the laying on of hands and sent with financial support to minister in Christ's name among the nations. When the Christian missionary has secret sins, such behavior ruins his reputation. It turns the trust-filled relationship that exists between the missionary and his partners into a mockery. His hypocrisy also has the potential to cause the people he has gone to serve to blaspheme Christ.

What about the third case study? Bob and Sue didn't start living a life of secret sin. They slid gradually into apostasy. Their struggle was intellectual at first. They didn't believe in the inerrancy of Scripture.

One might wonder whether or not their denial of the faith could have been avoided had they maintained their spiritual vitality as I've described it in this chapter. Wasn't spiritual vitality what Sue was seeking when she fasted for more than forty days while waiting on God to do something miraculous?

Their story is troubling, and it shows that while Christians can maintain their spiritual vitality by praying and reading the Scriptures regularly, such activity assumes faith. We must believe that all Scripture is God breathed and able to be trusted (2 Tim. 3:16).

We all know from experience that no Christian is perfect. So I'm not suggesting in this chapter sinless perfection for either the layman or the missionary. Instead, I'm speaking about living according to the standard to which we have attained. The Christian life is a life of forward movement. It begins with repentance and faith in Christ. We are declared righteous through our faith and set on a forward-moving path, the path of sanctification. The final destination is glorification and conformity to the image of Christ. In the meantime, however, we are left to live moment-by-moment in fellowship with the Holy Spirit. As we walk with him, he helps us put off our old nature and put on the new. This is accomplished thought-by-thought and word-by-word. If we neglect this relationship by not praying constantly, if we fail to take every opportunity to internalize the Scriptures, we will drift slowly; and unless God in his mercy forbids it, we will fall. Therefore, maintaining our spiritual vitality is a must!

CHAPTER SIX

AXIOM TWO — KNOW THE CULTURE

Several years ago a new missionary family came to the field in order to be involved in translation work. Before coming overseas the husband had spent nine years in Bible school and seminary and a couple more at a school which focused on linguistics and culture. He was passionate about theology and was a fine preacher. One of the things that became obvious as I got to know him better was he didn't appreciate what he felt had been an overemphasis on cultural anthropology in the latter part of his training. He vehemently dismissed culture as a tool of Satan. "All we need to do is preach the Bible," he used to urge fervently. (I said "used to" because he didn't make it past that challenging first year overseas!)

Do you agree with his assessment? Is it wise for a missionary to preach the Bible while ignoring the cultural context of his listeners? I believe the gospel of Jesus Christ "is the power of God for the salvation of everyone who believes" (Rom. 1:16). Not only that, but preaching it is indispensible in so much as "faith comes from hearing the message, and the message is heard through the word of Christ" (Rom. 10:17).

Preaching the gospel of Jesus Christ is at the center of the missionary endeavor. On the other hand, it's important to realize that preaching is a form of communication. If we try to do it without becoming intimately acquainted with the language and culture of the listeners, either non-communication or miscommunication is bound to happen.

I've experienced non-communication many times while overseas. The most extreme case happened while I was working at our mission's office in the capital city before coming to Tanna in 2003. Michele and I were looking for an English-speaking church to attend with the kids. We visited a congregation led by an American missionary and his wife. I was excited about the pastor's zeal for evangelism. Every week he would lead groups into the city to distribute tracts and pamphlets inviting people to come watch Bible-based videos at designated times and locations.

One Friday afternoon I agreed to go to a village just outside of town and help with this work. We left and arrived at a community building. Children were playing marbles on the hard ground outside. Teenagers were playing soccer in a nearby field. When they saw us arrive, they stopped what they were doing and gathered excitedly around the truck, helping the pastor and me as we moved the electronic equipment inside.

After everything was set up, I situated myself in the rear of the building content to observe. The pastor gave a brief introduction in English. When he started the video, I recognized a large city in the United States as the setting. The language was in English with no subtitles or translation. While I don't recall the plot completely, I remember vividly the gruesome special effects which depicted a man dying and going to hell where worms ate his body. I watched as those children and teenagers stared with fascination and horror.

When the video finished, the pastor continued in English. He preached earnestly a message of repentance, urging all those who had just seen the video to come forward and escape the flames. When he caught my eye, he shouted in an encouraging tone for me to make my way to the front and pray with those who would respond. Not knowing what the people had understood from the video, I was reluctant and declined.

The following week we went even further out of town to a small community of Tannese men and women. At that point I hadn't been introduced to any Tannese people. We got there and set up a large screen. The pastor gave the same introduction in English and then showed the same video. I made my way over to a Tannese family gathered around their cooking fire. I sat down and began chatting with them in *Bislama*. As we shared roasted plantains, I began to ask them about the video. I wanted to know if it was communicating to those who were watching.

As it turned out the husband was a follower of John Frum. They knew several languages. *Nafe*, the language my family ended up working in, was their first language. They knew *Bislama* as well and used it a lot since they lived in town. They had both been taught in French at a Catholic mission during their childhood from grades 1-6, but they rarely used it. Neither of them were comfortable in English. They explained that very few of the Tannese sitting there could understand the video, but they were glad to have the pastor come and show it. They liked videos. It was free. They didn't have anything else to do on a Friday night.

That was the last time I went on such an evangelistic campaign with that pastor. In my judgment it simply wasn't communicating to the people he was trying to reach. I felt he would have been better served to either (a) restrict his outreach to the limited number of people who could really understand English, or (b) learn the national language and at least try to explain the cinemas and make an appeal using the Bible available in it. As it was his failure to appreciate the linguistic diversity in Vanuatu resulted in non-communication much of the time.

Miscommunication is also a challenge for the foreign missionary. For this reason he must pay close attention to the host culture where he is serving. Although I could tell many stories wherein I've miscommunicated, one story involving two good-intentioned, short-term missionaries comes to mind. It will illustrate the point I'm trying to make.

I had been on Tanna for nearly eight years when I heard someone announce during Sunday service that there were going to be some special meetings held the following week. Two foreign women with special gifts were going to have a short crusade and help people in the community. The sick were encouraged to come. Anyone who needed prayer was welcomed.

The meetings were to be held in an open field belonging to the chief who had invited them through the I-know-a-pastor-who-has-a-friend network. The weeds were cleared. A temporary shelter was erected with two chairs and a table at the front for the special guests. Woven mats were put on the ground for those who would come to listen. A toilet was dug in the forest and enclosed to ensure no embarrassing moments. It was close to a river where water could be fetched for washing.

On the first afternoon of meetings I went out with my daughter. We were running a cross-country circuit for exercise. As we approached the open field at the base of the mountain, we could hear guitars and loud singing. I decided to check it out.

When I got there, I saw two middle-aged woman among a handful of locals. Their accents gave them away. They had come from the Bible Belt in the United States. I went and sat down on the woven mats with friends from the Presbyterian congregation.

The singing finished. Then the itinerant preachers began to share their testimonies through an interpreter. It was obviously an emotional experience for both of them. They wept openly. Several times they declared the great love they had for the people of Tanna. When they began speaking about the dreams and visions the Lord had given them to share with the people, I felt a knot form in my stomach. I managed a quiet escape several minutes later.

The following afternoon I purposefully went to go visit these two women before the meetings started. They were living out of a small tent set up on the raised bamboo platform. We shook hands and began a cordial conversation about where they were from. They shared about their ministry. It entailed visiting Tanna a couple times a year for a couple weeks each time. Their focus was prayer. They had seen a chief in the area healed in response to it and were excited about the results. I shared with them about the ongoing work of translation and literacy in the language group.

The two women were very thoughtful. They gave me a couple colorful skirts for my wife. (Just months shy of our furlough, the previous four years of village life had ruined most of her clothes.) I took some sweets home to my kids. They also gave me bandages and antibiotic ointments which within a couple weeks would help tremendously in our small community. In the end, after we had exchanged email addresses, we said goodbye while asking God's blessing on one another .

One of the people who had been instrumental in opening the door for the coming of the two generous ladies was a friend named George. George was in his late twenties and had a reputation for being hard working like his father who had died the year before. He was living outside of his tribal land in an area his father had bought from a friend over forty years prior to that time. George had been part of the translation team until he was asked to step down for moral reasons.

George's problems had begun when he did something that offended the grown children of the man his father had bought their property from. One of them had a daughter who got pregnant. She said the baby was George's. George denied it publically while admitting privately that it probably was his. The result was a fight that would eventually lead the young lady's father all the way to the nation's supreme court in his effort to force George off the land their fathers had made a legal transaction over.

George made other enemies with the same sort of behavior, living with one woman after another, sending them back to their parents after deciding he didn't want them anymore. At the time, when the two aforementioned prayer warriors came through the area, someone set George's bamboo-thatch kitchen on fire and it burned to the ground. Saucepans, utensils, and assorted other things went up in flames, breaking the heart of George's aging mother. He was angry and understandably wanted to know who did it. Yet how could he find out? No one had seen what happened.

Clairvoyants play a major role in Tannese religion. These are men and women who display a keen gift for seeing the unseen. For the price of some *kava* or a chicken people can find out all sorts of things. What caused this man's sickness? Why did that young boy die? Who stole from my garden? Who caused the rain to spoil our circumcision ceremony? Speculating about such things is the fodder that keeps the rumor mill on Tanna incessantly working, and the local clairvoyants are often the ones adding fuel to the fires of suspicion and slander through their dreaming.

George felt lucky. Why go to a local clairvoyant when he had two foreign women on hand with "the gift"? He went to them and told them about the kitchen and asked them to pray for him. They did and added to their prayer "a word." They told George the first person he would meet on the road going back to his house that night was either the one responsible for the fire or one who had knowledge about who had started it. On his way home George crossed paths with one of the family members of the man whose daughter had said George was the father of her baby.

Fast forward two weeks. The two women had gone back home. The village leaders and area council met to talk about who had burned George's kitchen down. Were there any witnesses? No. Did anyone want to confess they had done it? No. But wait . . . George felt certain he knew who did it. Not only that, but he believed he had God on his side.

George vehemently accused the young man he had crossed paths with that afternoon. Though the man denied it, George insisted it was true. When asked by the village chiefs how he knew this, he went on to share about the witness given by the two women who had prayed for him. Thankfully, the judges in the case demanded eye witnesses and disallowed such speculation, even if it was given in Jesus' name.

A couple months later one of those missionary women was kind enough to write me an email informing me she was planning another trip. She asked if there was anything I needed to give her by way of a "heads up." I took it as an open door and shared with her all that had happened with George and her previous encounters with him.

I asked plainly in the email if it was this woman's intention to be viewed as a prophetess on Tanna. I reminded her they have lots of so-called prophets of a non-Christian variety on the island. Many people claim to have the power to divine the sorts of things she had told George. I encouraged her to be careful and not go beyond what is written in the Scriptures. I suggested she try to incorporate more Bible content in her messages through interpreters.

Both women wrote back and appreciated what I suggested, but when it came to George and the word they had shared with him, they were both bewildered. How could something like that happen? They hadn't intended for their words to be used in a court case to pin the blame on someone when there had been no witnesses to the burning.

Or was God really on George's side? If it could have been proven that the fire had been started in retaliation for George's immoral behavior, wouldn't God be on the side of the offended fathers and mothers of the girls? Wouldn't one of the fathers of the young women George was treating disrespectfully have been justified to pummel George for his behavior? Indeed, some of the local Tannese might have felt that a burned kitchen was an appropriate show of anger whoever it was. At least they had had the courtesy to burn it while George and his family were not in it.

In the end it would have helped those two women if they had been more familiar with Tannese culture and how the people use clairvoyants. If they had known, they might have been more cautious in how or what they shared with the people asking for prayer.

This story was a learning experience for them. I know it was for me. It reminded me again of just how important it is to make sure we understand the language and the culture of the people we are going to serve in Jesus' name. The more we know, the better equipped we will be to avoid non-communication and miscommunication.

Stapleton ranch house built in Aspen, Colorado in early 1900s

Visiting Valdez, Alaska while in the U.S. Air Force 1990-1994

Michele and I at our wedding 1997

All our belongings in three crates & two barrels sent to Vanuatu in 2001

The old mission house on the hill that was our home in 2001

Our first village home on Tanna 2003

Michele homeschooling David in village 2004

Visiting the bank and post office in Lenakel, Tanna

Tearing down our second village home on Tanna 2005

The beloved Toyota Landcruiser with flowers attached

Dedication of a New Testament in a neighboring language in 2007

Remains of Last Tree Church outside our front door after Cyclone Ivy Feb. 2004

Michele making laplap with friends

JohnMark and a fruit bat

Yasur Volcano explodes with local 4X4 transport in foreground

Grandfather Peter

Our final village home on Tanna built 2005

Our Mitsubishi high centered on a breadfruit tree

After I fell in the boat and came ashore in drama depicting the early missionaries' arrival

A young man from the John Frum Movement with "USA" painted on his chest

Working with mother-tongue speakers to facilitate the translation of the Nafe New Testament

Kwamera Presbyterian Church as it stood for nearly a decade while being built with nickel-and-dime offerings

A heap of taro and other gifts to pay a bride price

The quad bike my Tannese friends felt was a selfish purchase

CHAPTER SEVEN

AXIOM THREE — DON'T OFFEND UNNECESSARILY

The foreign missionary should try not to offend unnecessarily. Someone reading this third axiom is bound to disagree with it. They will argue that the Christian missionary can't avoid being offensive. The Lord Jesus offended the religious leaders of his day by proclaiming the truth. His apostles offended people through their preaching. The Scriptures teach us the gospel of Jesus Christ is "a stumbling block to Jews and foolishness to Gentiles" (1 Cor. 1:23). If we proclaim it like we are commanded to do, some people are bound to get angry.

The above argument is true, and this axiom isn't talking about avoiding confrontation or the potential conflict which arises from preaching the gospel to antagonistic people. Instead, it's dealing with interpersonal relationships. It assumes that each person possesses within himself a sense of what constitutes proper, normal behavior. This internal sense has been conditioned more by culture than by moral absolutes, and for this reason it differs from one person to another.

The foreign missionary works in a different culture with people from many different backgrounds. This lack of homogeneity is a recipe for strife, but the missionary doesn't want to have relationships marked by hurt feelings and misunderstanding. For this reason he needs to be sensitive to the opinions of others and avoid doing things that will offend them unnecessarily.

OFFENDING BY OUR SPEECH

I have worked for many years with Australians in Vanuatu. One day I was talking with one of them. My youngest son Joel was nearby and I affectionately called him "little bugger." My Australian friend cringed. When I asked what was wrong, he explained that "bugger" was vulgar slang in Australian English. Needless to say, I stopped using that term around him lest I offend him unnecessarily.

I had to begin teaching my children at an early age to avoid using certain words in the vernacular language on Tanna because they were swear words. It wasn't because the words had any negative emotional meaning for my kids. When they were young, they could've said those words without feeling they were doing something wrong because English was their mother tongue and not *Nafe.* Yet for the sake of their playmates I still had to correct them at times. I didn't want them to offend unnecessarily.

OFFENDING BY OUR GESTURES

I was walking in Lenakel one afternoon when I saw an older gentleman from the language community walking on the other side of the road. He waved at me. I smiled and pointed my finger straight at him. He approached me with an unhappy look on his face. He scolded me for pointing at him like a person accusing him of a crime. Then he asked me not to do it again. I was surprised and apologized profusely.

In America sticking one's middle finger up is an offensive gesture. If I were walking down the street in my home country and someone signaled me to come by sticking his middle finger up while moving it back and forth at the middle knuckle, I would be offended. I might excuse a foreigner for doing it, but I would undoubtedly ask him not to do it again.

OFFENDING BY OUR ACTIONS

Angry protests in the Middle East are often shown on the television in America. The mob sometimes expresses anger by burning American flags. That behavior is offensive to Americans and could be avoided for the sake of trying to promote peace. In the same way emotions get enflamed when Muslims hear about American pastors burning Korans. Is the Koran true? Christians believe no. Yet the way to reach Muslims isn't by treating their sacred objects as profane.

When my children were young and their consciences still very impressionable, they would often come home from going to the garden with friends in Tanna. They would share with me over evening devotions the things they had been told. Don't cut that vine! Don't spit here! Don't urinate there! If you do that the spirits will hurt you!

I didn't realize how much my children were being influenced by these animistic assertions their friends had been making. It was revealed to me one afternoon when my family was working near our house. We were gathering firewood when my daughter pointed to a large stone hidden in the roots of a tree. "Daddy, don't touch that!" she said. Her brothers were standing to the side and began telling me what their friends had said about this sacred stone.

On a quiet day when no one was in the village I went to where the large stone was and picked it up. My children's eyes were round as saucers as I put it down and sat on it. I explained to them the biblical teaching about idolatry. I said there was no power in those stones except in the minds of those who believed in them.

What do you think? Should I have done that in front of the whole village? If I had done that, undoubtedly there would have been some quiet opposition against me and my family from custom chiefs steeped in their animistic ways. So I was faced with the question of necessity. I decided it wasn't something I had to do. I felt it would be more productive in the long run to be allowed to keep the peace, stay in the village, finish the Bible translation, and then let those words speak authoritatively about the errors of reverencing holy stones and places as though they had the power to save or destroy.

I went to the bank in Lenakel one Friday. It was payday and the line was long. I was standing patiently with forty other people. The wait would be about an hour. Suddenly a couple of my zealous countrymen on a short-term mission trip came to the door. One of them was wearing a shirt which had a large picture on it of Jesus dying on the cross. The other was wearing a hat that said "Jesus is Lord!"

Without a thought these two middle-aged men moved to the front of the line and pulled out a wad of American dollars. As the woman behind the counter exchanged their money, I could hear the rumblings of discontent going on around me. The girl next to me fumed to her friend between gritted teeth, saying, "Hey! If we were in their country we wouldn't be allowed to do that."

After the two men got their money, they left smiling. The one with the hat looked over his shoulder as he passed out the door. "God bless!" he shouted.

Those two men had rudely cut in front of forty people and then had the audacity to pronounce a blessing. That was an awkward moment for me, a foreigner living among the Tannese. Yet there was a moment I endured which was even more awkward than that one.

OFFENDING BY OUR (ACTIONS AND) CLOTHES

On a different day I had stopped for lunch at a popular bamboo-thatch restaurant located in the middle of Lenakel. A large open window had been constructed into the seaside wall. While enjoying their meals, patrons could sit and look out at the ocean waves as they rolled gently onto the beach.

The tables were full when I showed up. I was eating my fish soup over rice when suddenly the Tannese men around me began chattering while looking out the window. Curious to know what all the buzz was about, I put my fork down, turned, and nearly choked on a fishbone.

The easily-visible beach was deserted except for a Caucasian young man standing in stomach-high water with his lover. She was dressed in a two-piece bikini. Her legs were wrapped around his waist and her arms around his neck. He was holding her up in the water by her bottom. They might have been newlyweds or something. I don't know. Whoever they were, my face turned bright red as I tried to ignore the conversation going on around me.

"Hmm," the first Tannese man grunted.

"What are they doing?" his friend asked.

"No," a third man spoke dismissively. "It's their love. It's their way."

The men laughed and made jokes about the couple until I couldn't handle it any longer. I finished my food and went down to the water.

"Excuse me," I said.

The woman separated herself from the man, and the two of them turned my way. "G'day," they both said with a Commonwealth accent.

What to say now? I wondered. It was too late for me to stop. "Hope you are enjoying your vacation," I went on. "You might not know it, but right now you two are the laughing stock of everyone up on the hill there." I pointed to the restaurant and the other stores where people were still standing around gawking.

The man said, "Ooh, I was wondering about that."

I replied, "Well, for what it's worth, the Tannese are much more reserved in their public displays of affection. I can't tell you what you can and cannot do, but you might consider being a little more modest in public."

I felt truly sorry for that young woman as she realized what had been going on in the minds of the numerous people looking down on them. She was in a two-piece bikini, but as she came blushing out of the water she might as well have been naked. She quickly covered herself with a towel and the two of them skulked away feeling embarrassed and ashamed. Yet those feelings could've been avoided had the two of them tried a little harder to be more like the people in the country they were visiting both with their choice of clothes and their conduct toward one another.

Offending by What We Eat and Drink

I've already made the point that consuming *kava* is an important part of the daily lives of Tannese men. In fact, it's often the first topic of conversation that comes up when I meet new people.

They want to know whether or not I'm a *kava* drinker.

In all my years in Tanna I've never tasted *kava*. There are two reasons. First, it's difficult for me to drink another man's saliva voluntarily. Second, I try to live by the apostle Paul's exhortation. He said we shouldn't make a fellow Christian stumble by what we eat or drink (1 Cor. 10:31-32). Several Christian denominations on Tanna frown on *kava* drinking. For the sake of their consciences I abstain from doing so.

When I was on Santo Island back in 2001, I had gone to the town of Luganville on a hot day. My shirt was sticky with sweat as I walked down the main street. Inside one store I saw the refrigerator full of ice-cold beer. Now I have many Presbyterian friends who are happy to drink beer in moderation. At the same time, however, I have many Baptist friends who won't touch it. For me, to drink or not to drink is purely a matter of conscience. I'm no better off if I do drink; I'm no better off if I don't. Only drunkenness is forbidden in the Scriptures (Eph. 5:18). On this occasion I did drink a single beer and felt refreshed. It cooled me off and made the rest of the afternoon bearable.

Several weeks later I was discussing such matters with a church elder in the village where we were living. He asked about alcohol, and I shared with him the same sort of theology expressed above. I spoke hypothetically, "Yes, I could drink a beer. It wouldn't make me dirty in God's eyes." The elder agreed with me, but he kindly suggested if I did drink alcohol I shouldn't do it in front of anyone. If I did, they wouldn't believe in the translation work we had been sent to help with. Since that time I've avoided consumption of alcohol while working in Vanuatu.

The above stories illustrate an important lesson for you, the hopeful missionary. Do you want to have good relationships with people from different cultures while you are living overseas? If you do, you must recognize that each person possesses a culturally conditioned sense of proper behavior. While their sense of propriety can't be the law that absolutely governs the way you act, you will do well to take their opinions into consideration while interacting with them and avoid offending them unnecessarily with things like your speech, your gestures, your actions, your clothes, and the things you eat and drink.

CHAPTER EIGHT

AXIOM FOUR — AVOID THE PEDDLING - THE-GOSPEL-FOR-PROFIT PERCEPTION

Missionaries aren't unlike other people. They need money to provide for both their physical needs and the material needs of the ministry they are involved in. Several common ministry models are followed to provide these necessary funds. The model you choose will depend upon your personal preferences, the preferences of your sending church, the official policy of the organization you affiliate yourself with (if indeed you affiliate yourself with a particular organization), and the laws of the government in the country where you plan to serve.

The first ministry model is the tent-making model. This model gets its name from the example of the apostle Paul, who was a tentmaker together with Aquila and Priscilla (Acts 18:1-4). The Christian missionary following this model works fulltime to provide for his physical needs while taking every opportunity to spread the gospel of Christ. In some closed countries tent-making ministry is the only viable option since Christian missionaries aren't allowed to work openly.

The second ministry model is the faith-based model. The foreign missionary following this model doesn't work fulltime to provide for his physical needs. He depends on churches and individuals to meet them. They send financial gifts through the mission board on a monthly, quarterly, or spontaneous basis. The faith-based missionary is free to work fulltime at spreading the gospel of Christ in the country where he is serving.

The faith-based model has more than one form. The first form of the faith-based ministry model is followed by missionaries sent as representatives of a particular denomination, and the denomination assumes the responsibility of providing for their financial needs. It isn't necessary for these missionaries to go on deputation and seek individuals and churches to partner with them directly. Their salary is fixed and guaranteed once they become members of their church's mission board.

While some don't include this paradigm in the faith-based model, I prefer to think of it that way because there still exists a faith element in it. The funds are ultimately given by church members whose financial situations change. For this reason both those who give and the missionary receiving the funds must look to the Lord in faith, believing he will provide for their needs consistently.

Another form of faith-based missions is followed by the Christian missionary whose salary isn't guaranteed. The missionary living in this manner depends upon a core group of churches and individuals who have committed to give regularly as the Lord provides. The monthly income of the missionary following this form fluctuates from month to month. This is the form of faith-based missions my family and I have participated in during our time overseas.

A third model in the faith-based paradigm was seen in people like Gladys Aylward. A young woman who went to work in China in

1932, Gladys had been turned down by the China Inland Mission (Tucker, Kindle Locations 6573-6575). When she left her home in England, she wasn't attached to any mission board. She had only her train ticket and very little money. The Lord rewarded her faith by caring for her needs in a variety of ways over a long career in missions.

Gladys Aylward showed real courage and determination. Her method was noble to be sure. Some undoubtedly have followed in her footsteps and seen God reward their faith. In this book, however, I assume most of you will receive regular support from your denomination or from a group of churches and individuals through a mission board.

Now if you are from an industrialized nation planning to follow the faith-based model while working in an "underdeveloped" country, you need to realize something. The people living in those countries generally don't have a lot of money. Your annual income will likely be many times higher than theirs. This will be true even if your annual income is below the average income of the people in your station of life back in your home country.

Case in point, in Vanuatu the minimum wage is less than the equivalent of $2.00 USD an hour. None of the people in the village where we live have regular paying jobs. They survive by gardening every day. On the odd occasion when they decide to hire a truck to take them to the market in town, they might make money equal to about $40-$50 USD. Otherwise they get by without even the most basic commodities like toilet paper and dish soap. To these humble people, an average tax return for a middleclass American family of six would be an unimaginable amount.

Because a large financial gap will likely exist between you and the people you will be serving,[2] it's important to think through the implications of such a reality and be prepared to adjust your lifestyle accordingly. The last thing you want is to be perceived by others as peddling the gospel of Christ for profit.

During my undergraduate studies I was shown a video in one of my classes preparing me for foreign missions. I don't recall which class it was. I can't remember the name of the video. What I do recall is the sour taste it left in my mouth as I watched it.

The video had been produced by a secular anthropologist attempting to smear the evangelistic efforts of the Church in a country where the people lived primitively. He interviewed several Christian missionaries from industrialized nations, asking them probing questions into their worldview. Do you believe these people are going to hell? Is Jesus the only way to God? Is the culture of this people from the Devil?

The anthropologist asked inflammatory questions like these then edited the audio to make the answers sound as ungracious as possible. As the audio ran, the camera panned out and showed pictures detailing the situations these missionaries lived in. Care was taken to paint an ugly picture.

The video insinuated that the missionaries were living like kings among their subjects. They had richly built homes while the

---

[2] Because wealth is culturally defined, it's impossible to speak about money and missionaries using a cookie-cutter approach. The culture the missionary is from, the needs of the missionary and his or her family, the kind of ministry they are involved in, the official support quota approved by their mission board, and many things like these make each situation unique.

people around them lived in grass houses. The missionaries slept in waterbeds while the nationals slept on dirt floors. The missionaries had all the modern amenities while the people had nothing. The expansive yards of the missionaries were well-kept by poorly paid locals pushing lawnmowers. Photo after incriminating photo was shown as this secular anthropologist indirectly accused these missionaries of peddling the gospel for profit while taking advantage of the poor.

On one occasion I had gone to Lenakel and was checking my email. While online I visited a popular news website. One of the main articles spoke disparagingly about the owners of a large Christian broadcasting company. A husband and his wife, the two of them had made millions of tax free, non-profit dollars. The article described their fancy cars, the mansions they owned, the large Christian-based theme park they had constructed, and the conflicts the money had caused in their family.

After I read the article, I thought about the the author's intent. He hadn't written that piece of journalism to inform. It was a scathing accusation of Judas-like behavior. That Christian couple had been stealing from the non-profit money bag in order to satisfy their own appetite for opulent living.

One morning before a meeting the members of our mission sat down to watch a taped sermon preached by a popular American pastor. This pastor had published several Christian books. The royalties had made him huge sums of money. He was preaching about ministry when suddenly he divulged that he and his wife had made a practice of giving away 90% of their income to charity.

Jesus said when we give we aren't to let our left hand know

what our right hand is doing. Our giving is to be done in secret so our Father who sees in secret might reward us (Matt. 6:3-4). So why did this influential pastor feel it was important to announce to the world that he and his wife were such magnanimous givers? While it's not my place to judge him, I can speculate. Probably some people had been accusing him of peddling the gospel of Christ for profit. He felt it was important to justify himself. He had indeed made large sums of money by means of that gospel, but he wanted those people to know he was giving most of it away.

It's important to remind ourselves all the time that Christian service is not like a secular career. The chief aim is not financial profit. When the Lord Jesus called his first disciples to follow him, he told them the price tag for such service would be high. They would be leaving parents and extended family and homes and lands in order to go and preach the gospel. Would their needs be cared for in this life? Yes. Yet their final reward, the one worth sacrificing for, was to come in the future with the arrival of God's glorious, eternal kingdom (Luke 18:28-30).

This still begs the question: if you are from an industrialized nation planning to be a missionary living in a poor country, and if your support quota will likely be higher than the income of the average person in that country, how can you avoid people perceiving you as someone peddling the gospel of Christ for profit? The answer to that question isn't easy.

In one sense it will be impossible for you to explain your motives and needs to everyone. By way of example let me share another story that took place in the bank in Lenakel.

I was waiting in line when Sarah, one of the tellers, smiled and motioned with her head that it was my turn to step up to the counter. I pulled out my wallet and went. The two of us made small talk as I filled out a withdrawal form. I requested money equal to about $250 USD. I needed to buy some natural gas for our stove. I needed fresh fish from the market, some beef, several root crops, fruits, and other assorted odds and ends Michele had added to my weekly list of groceries.

Sarah took the form and began typing on her computer. When my account information appeared, her eye got wide with surprise. She began processing my withdrawal and continued our casual conversation.

"Mr. Erik, how much do you spend every month in the village where you live?"

Being from a country where speaking about one's salary is a taboo thing even between close friends and family members, I was shocked. *All she has to do is observe the pattern of our monthly deposits,* I thought. *Why ask me? That was rude.*

"Oh, it depends," I said evasively. "Sometimes we spend more and sometimes less."

As Sarah signed off on my withdrawal slip and began counting out the money I was requesting, I suddenly realized what had made her ask about our expenses. I had recently made a deposit equal to about $1000 USD.

"Sarah, did you see I put a large deposit in last week?" I asked.

She nodded her head and looked at me, waiting for me to continue explaining the presence of what must have seemed a fortune to her.

I obliged her and said, "I've been saving some money every month for some time now. I was keeping it in the village, but since a neighbor recently had some money stolen from his house, I brought it to the bank. That money is for a special purpose, and I need to keep saving."

"What is the money for?" Sarah asked inquisitively.

"It's for a medical procedure I want to have done on my daughter. She needs to have metal put on her teeth to straighten them."

Well, when I got those words out, Sarah's face went blank. Very expensive metal things put on teeth to straighten them? Thankfully she didn't inquire further. She simply gave me my money and offered me a nice day while welcoming me to come back next time.

In all my years in Tanna I've never seen a Tannese person with braces on their teeth. What I've seen is quite the opposite: children with rotting permanent teeth, adults with a large gap where their two front teeth used to be, and lots of teeth stained black from tobacco and/or flattened from chewing too much *kava*. In Tanna few people brush their teeth. Floss is an unknown piece of merchandise.

With that culture as a background it wouldn't have mattered what I said to Sarah. It's unlikely I would have been able to make her feel in her heart that saving such a large amount of money wasn't extravagant. I might have tried, of course. I could've explained that young people in my home culture get braces in middle school. Young women in my home culture are pressured to have straight, beautiful smiles. I want to do whatever is within my means to help my daughter have a positive feeling about her physical appearance since she will probably live long term in that environment. Whether or not Sarah would have been able to appreciate my reasoning is another matter.

Although in some cases it will be impossible to avoid people perceiving you negatively because of your finances, there is something you can do that will help people be more apt to view your rich heritage with warmth rather than scorn. What is it? you ask. You can be generous.

Generosity is highly esteemed among the Tannese people. I remember one occasion when this was brought home to me in a vivid way. A friend in the village had been married for several years. He and his wife had three beautiful children. The time came for him to pay his in-laws what amounted to a bride price. The exchange would seal the deal and make it virtually impossible for my friend's wife to return to her father's house no matter what marital problems might arise.

On the day of this important ceremony many people came to the village. My friend led me and several men to his garden. We made trip after trip carrying bundles of root crops. When we got to the place where the ceremony was to be held, the bundles were heaped up in a pile as tall as a full-grown man. On top of the pile blankets and mats and pieces of cloth were spread twenty layers thick. Bundles of sugarcane were placed around the heap. A goat was tethered to the side of it. A cow was killed. Several tuber puddings had been prepared and were divided and given out.

Later that afternoon I was asked to drive all this food to the village of the woman's family. I agreed and had to tell the people no one could sit in the back of the truck because the load was so heavy. I drove down the mountain with my friend's brother-in-law. When we got to his house, he told me to back up and put the tailgate near an open door. I did so, and this man began to throw all that food into an empty room filled with disposable things like old newspapers and used building materials.

"This is a lot of food," I observed.

"Yes," the man agreed. "We will never be able to eat it all before it rots."

I was shocked thinking of the waste. "Why then do you do this ceremony?" I asked.

The man laughed. "It's our custom," he said.

I shook my head in wonder at this action. It displayed so clearly the importance of generosity in the culture on Tanna. It certainly trumped the value of being resourceful with food.

The importance of generosity comes out in the way the Tannese speak, too. For example, when a person talks about his personal possessions, he is careful to use the appropriate possessive pronouns, including the listener as one of the owners. Instead of "my ball" it's "our ball." Rather than "my spear gun" it's "our spear gun." They use it for nearly everything.

During our first term on Tanna we purchased a rusty 1971 Toyota Landcruiser. The second term we bought a 2001 Mitsubishi 4X4 truck. On both occasions, on the first day we drove those vehicles into the village, people cheered and threw flowers. They were so excited to have a means of transportation nearby. It comforted them in their isolation. If they needed to get to town when my family was going, they could jump on. If there was an emergency, they would have a quick way to the hospital. For six years we helped with such emergencies. The people loved us for it. Always they were eager to say thanks for "our truck," including both us and themselves in that possessive pronoun.

The roads on Tanna are horrible. I endured them for six years before deciding I had had enough. I was tired of broken vehicles and the expense to keep them running. I also felt driving back and forth to town was taking too much time away from the translation work. The people would have to depend upon other means of transportation meager as they were.

I sold our Mitsubishi truck before our third furlough. While back in the United States for a year I didn't ask our supporting churches and friends for funds to purchase a replacement. Instead, when I returned to the field, I used the money from the sale of the truck to purchase a two-person, 4X4 ATV. I bought it in Port Vila after returning to the field and sent it to Tanna on a ship.

I'd like to forget the first day I drove that four-wheeler from the wharf up the dirt road in the middle of town to the market. It was an unusual sight to see since only a handful of people owned them on Tanna. Strangers looked at me with cold stares. When I drove around the island to our home, the people in our village heard the engine and came running. I got to the last gate and looked into bewildered faces. There were no cheers. No flowers flew through the air. "Oh, Missi Erik," they said. "Look at your small motorcycle you bought for yourself."

For several months after that day I tried to make people happy. Every conversation I had, when the topic came to the ATV, I was careful to refer to it as "our motorcycle," including the listeners in the possessive pronoun. They always replied with "your motorcycle." I got the politely spoken message. They thought I had been greedy and self-serving in purchasing it.

In the end I found small ways to help with that ATV. Yet the whole incident made me recall again how important it is for the foreign missionary to understand how his use of personal finances can influence other people's opinion of him and the work he is doing. The circumspect missionary must appreciate this; and even though he might be misunderstood at times and fail to please everyone with his decisions, he should do all he can in a culturally appropriate way to avoid the peddling-the-gospel-for-profit perception.

CHAPTER NINE

AXIOM FIVE — MAKE INCARNATIONAL MINISTRY YOUR GOAL

The foreign missionary should make every effort to be engaged in incarnational ministry. This statement is true. It also requires a bit of explanation since sincere Christians understand different things when using the popular word "incarnate" in its various forms. Let me define my use of it here.

The word "incarnate" is a Middle English word derived from Latin *in* and *caro* (Unger, 613). It means "to make flesh." In theology the noun form "incarnation" is used to refer to what our Lord Jesus did when he unselfishly considered our needs above his own. He is God, but he set aside his divine glory and was made flesh. Jesus Christ is God condescended and revealed as a man (Phil. 2:5-7).

Given the primary theological use of the term, some people have objected to the use of it as an adjective describing a kind of ministry. They reason rightly that Christians shouldn't make an unbiblical distinction among people. For example, if by the term "incarnational ministry" a person intends to imply the minister is somehow majestically superior in his person or culture, thus requiring him to condescend and help inferior, needy people, that is wrong and can be felt by others as pejorative.

It's true the missionary leaves his home. His home might

have more financial wealth and "progress" than the place where he has gone to serve. This might make the missionary feel he has set aside the privileges of his birth and condescended to go serve in that place. The people in the host country might have physical and spiritual needs that are more apparent than those of the missionary's countrymen. All those things are true, but it's still possible for that missionary to go overseas and not accomplish the goal of incarnational ministry.

So what do I understand by the term? It's only this: The missionary engaged in incarnational ministry lives among the people he is serving in Christ's name. He learns their language. He comes to understand their culture and worldview. As much as possible he becomes an insider and gets intimately involved in the lives of the people.

It must be admitted that incarnational ministry as I have defined it here isn't always possible. Sometimes uncontrollable factors militate against it, things like political instability, visa restrictions, and opposition to the work. Yet in an ideal situation the missionary needs to be in a place for an extended period. He needs to be able to lay the foundation for what will hopefully be successful communication in the future.[3]

If the missionary is able to live for an extended period with the people he is serving in Christ's name, he needs to be prepared to

---

[3] This is certainly true for missionaries engaged in the work of Bible translation. When the missionary is the one translating, which does happen more or less in places with very low education, the burden to know the language and culture is heavier. For the missionary who advises national translators who have better education, knowing the language and the culture helps him in his work as well.

live differently than he had become accustomed to living in his home country. The degree of difference will depend of course upon how different the two cultures are. In my family's case, our home culture and the host culture were worlds apart. Let me tell you the story of what it was like to make the move to live among the Tannese.

In 2003 I had to go ahead of my family to make preparations for their arrival in the village where we would live for the next decade. A large group of exuberant locals had gathered when I arrived. They surrounded me and the Presbyterian pastor and the village chiefs who were showing me the way to the house they had built for us.

The house was different on the outside. A tiny structure measuring about 108 square feet, it had been constructed with woven bamboo on the walls. The roof was dried coconut leaves fastened with vines to crooked rafters. Two small windows had been cut into the side of the house. The center pieces that swung in and out had been made with timber cut with a chain saw. They were hinged with animal hide and old pieces of a tire. The front door had been built for a local about five feet tall. In fact, the whole structure had been built by default for a person that size.

The inside of the house was different, too. The floor was dirt. The people had covered it with disposable, coconut-leaf mats. Two chest-high partitions had been erected with woven bamboo, dividing the house into three equal, tiny rooms. The builders had reasoned one room for me and my wife, one for our two boys, and one for our little girl. Inside those rooms there were no shelves, no beds, no dressers, just the materials that gave this little house an earthy feel. As I stood inspecting it for the first time, it felt to me like it had grown up out of the tropical soil on its own.

The people had become quiet as I inspected the inside. When I stepped back outside with a smile, saying, "Oh, thank you all very much," one of the older men gained courage by it. He took my arm and pulled me excitedly toward the side of the house where a shallow embankment rolled down into dense, tropical forest. "There is your small house," he said, pointing to the pit toilet they had dug and sheltered with the same materials they had constructed the house with.

The people went on to show me other different things. Our village was situated at the base of a large mountain about a twenty minute walk up a gradual incline from the ocean. World Vision had installed a long plastic pipe several years earlier. It brought water from a natural spring located several miles away toward the mountain's peak. It fed the water into two large cement tanks in the *tanirua*, or the ground outside where the villagers' cows and pigs roamed free. Another pipe fed water to a neighbor's house. A naked spigot was attached to a piece of wood. I was told my family and I could shower there.

I took lots of pictures and video on that day. When I got back to the capital city, I showed Michele. Her eyes got wide. "Wow," she managed.

"It's okay, honey," I said. "We can turn that house into the kitchen. We can build a sleeping house a little bit bigger behind it."

"Can you make a washroom where we can shower in private?" she asked.

"I think so," I agreed.

"Oh, and we need a place to do laundry," she pleaded. "And

where are you going to work?"

That first house did indeed become our kitchen. We built another house with the same local materials just behind it. It was a single room about twice the size of the first one. We put a large tarp on the floor to help keep our feet clean. We also hung plastic on the roof just under the coconut leaves. This helped keep the rodents out of sight and blocked rotting leaves and lizard droppings from falling on our stuff. Michele got her washroom, and I constructed a small office that later became a toolshed.

My family lived in that single-room house with the separate kitchen for about 30 months while we learned the vernacular language and the local culture and worldview on a fulltime basis. It wasn't easy to live that way. It was uncomfortable. Yet the Lord used it in our lives to teach us many biblical principles. Simplicity, contentment, and being grateful for small things like a welcomed change in the weather or running water were just a few of the lessons.

Incarnational ministry has the power to break down the walls of fear and prejudice. I saw this in the life of one of the old men in our village, Grandfather Peter. His clan had adopted my family. Our house was on his property. One afternoon during our first year in the village, I went to the *nakamal* during *kava* drinking time in order to record some vernacular stories. This old man shared his perceptions of how those walls had come down. This is a translation of what he said:

> Before, when we were living in this place, a long time before at the time of our ancestors, we were living and hadn't seen you a foreigner before arriving and living in this place.

Suppose it was before when we were living here had we seen you we would have been afraid of you. The ancestors would have been afraid of you. But now, it's a changed time, it's a new time now we are living in it. We walk together, and eat together, and talk together. One more point is this. Before, when the ancestors were living, they didn't know that you all would come and arrive at this place, the place where we live in darkness. But now you, a foreigner, have arrived and come to this place, the room of our ancestors. Our ancestors aren't here anymore, and we see you living here in our midst now. Sometime the ancestors will exist, they will look this way, they will see we are living here, but it's a changed time,
you a foreigner you are living in our midst.

Incarnational ministry breaks down walls of fear and prejudice, but that is not all. It also opens hearts by placing the missionary in a context where genuine friendships can be made. Those friendships having been established, it then provides opportunities for sharing the gospel of Christ in a non-artificial way. Grandfather Peter taught me those lessons as well.

My friendship with Grandfather Peter had begun soon after our arrival in the village. He used to pass by our house on his way to and from his garden every day. Often times on his way home in the early afternoon he would stop to give us some sweet potatoes, some long stocks of sugarcane, or a bundle of bananas. We would then share something from our pantry in return. His favorite was pumpkin cake Michele had learned to bake in a small Coleman stove.

Grandfather Peter was a courageous man. In February 2004 Cyclone Ivy passed over our end of the island. It was a direct hit. The wind sounded like a loud freight train. It blew non-stop for twenty-four hours, shaking our little house on its freshly planted posts. In the middle of the night Michele and I were praying and comforting our frightened children when suddenly there was a loud knock on the door. Several kids with their parents were standing outside seeking refuge. Their homes had been built a couple years before ours so the cyclone blew them down easily. I invited them to squeeze inside and sit with us. When I asked about Grandfather Peter, the people shook their heads. "One side of his house has fallen," they said, "but he told us to leave him sleeping by his fire. If he dies there he will die there!"

Grandfather Peter was a very unassuming person. When I returned to the village after furlough in 2005, I had gone ahead of the family again to get things ready for our newborn son, Joel. Grandfather Peter was next to our yard to greet me. Only something had changed. I was shocked.

"Grandfather Peter, what happened to your eye?" I asked

"Oh, that," he said, pointing to a glass eye in his eye socket. "I was brushing away leaves when a coconut spline poked my eyeball. It got infected. The doctor had to take it out."

I stood there imagining the familiar scene. He had wounded his eye. Rather than go straight to the doctor, he had chosen custom medicine. This meant people had spit various chewed-up leaves in his face. Perhaps they had mixed the leaves into water for him to drink. His eye most likely could've been saved had he simply gone to get some antibiotic ointment or drops. Yet this humble man had taken the loss as though it were simply a loose tooth that had come out.

Three years later I was working in my office when a group of yelling children ran by. I went to the door and asked one of them what was happening. He said Grandfather Peter had fallen on the garden path. They were going to see if he was alright.

I followed quickly behind and found Grandfather Peter being held up by several of his grandchildren. He was unconscious, and no one knew what to do. Not being a doctor, their guess was as good as mine. I came in close and prayed with them. We agreed to take turns carrying him to the village. I went first, carrying his fragile frame piggyback. I could feel his labored breathing as we moved slowly along.

We got Grandfather Peter back to the translation office and sat him on the couch. By that time he was semi-conscious, rambling incoherently. Several of his extended family began spitting chewed up leaves on him, speaking incantations. I prayed again with them. Five minutes passed and then Grandfather Peter died in the quiet, humble manner in which he had lived. "My grandchildren, I think I'm going to be leaving you now." Those had been his last words.

My heart broke for Grandfather Peter. I felt a sense of genuine loss. There was nothing artificial about it when on the next day his family asked me to share from the Scriptures and pray before burying him. I felt privileged, and before the many people who had gathered to grieve this well-known old man, the Lord opened a door to share his gospel. It was familiar to some. Yet to the many still very animistic in their worldview, it was another seed planted that I pray by God's grace will one day bear the fruit of genuine salvation and life change.

Sometime later I was asked by a pastor in a neighboring village to come preach. I took the recently published vernacular translation of the book of Acts. The message was about the seven sons of Sceva who tried to cast out demons without having a relationship with Jesus Christ (Acts 19:13-20). During the service I pointed out that many people on Tanna are thoroughly animistic in their worldview, but they are pleased to attempt to use Jesus' name once their magic has failed. It doesn't work because those people don't have a genuine relationship with the Savior.

After the service was over, I was sitting down with several of the church members. I listened as they began to speak to one another about their animistic beliefs, or "kastom" as they called it. They were perplexed about how deeply rooted it was in their daily lives. One minute they were shaking their heads in sorrow. The next they were laughing raucously, pointing out examples of people who had behaved like Sceva's sons. Suddenly the chief looked at me.

"Missi Erik," he said. "You and your family have come to live with us. Your skin is not the same color as ours, but you are one of us. You speak our language, and you know our customs. We cannot hide them from you. We invite you to tell us whenever you see something in our lives that is not straight with what the Bible says."

I was quick to admit to this chief that he and his people had already taught me and my family a great deal by the humble lives they were living in community. Nonetheless, I accepted his invitation to preach freely in the event I saw things inconsistent with the Bible.

What an invitation, huh! Why was it extended to me? My family and I were invited to speak frankly with that community because they regarded us as insiders. We lived with them, and the walls of fear and prejudice had come down. Hearts had been opened. We knew their language, culture, and worldview. That's incarnational ministry, and that ought to be the goal of the Christian missionary as he looks to the Lord to change hearts through his witness.

CHAPTER TEN

AXIOM SIX — LOVE THE PEOPLE BY EATING THEIR FOOD

At the beginning of one of my courses on missions during my undergraduate studies, the professor said, "If you love me, you will love my food." It was asserted repeatedly throughout the course as an assumed fact which needed no proof. It became so familiar that friends eating in the student dining hall would repeat it as a joke while forking unwanted items like tomatoes from one plate to another.

On the last day of the course the professor stood in front of the class. A basket of what appeared to be hard-boiled eggs was on the table before him. He cracked one open and began to eat it. Only it wasn't a normal egg. It had a half developed embryo inside, complete with a beak and tiny feathers. "This is a Pilipino delicacy called *balut*," the professor explained. Then he passed around the basket, inviting the students to try some.

That dish was strange to most (if not all) of the students in that particular class. Passing it around was part of our final exam. It wasn't graded of course, but it was memorable. Had we truly come to understand? If we wanted to lovingly embrace a people to serve them in Christ's name, this would mean embracing them with their culinary habits, even if they were a lot different than our own. On that day only a few students passed that part of the test. The rest declined with quiet expressions like "Eww!", "Yuck!", and "Hmm, no thanks."

The Bible doesn't actually articulate verbatim this love-me-love-my-food axiom. It has to be inferred from stories like the one in Acts 10:11-16. The Old Testament dietary laws had separated the Jews and the Gentiles for centuries. The word "unclean" had become not only an adjective describing various foods but a derogatory term to refer to the Gentile nations who ate them. Issues like food laws and circumcision rites created great hostility between the two groups.

It was in this context the apostle Peter saw a vision. A large sheet was let down from the sky by its four corners. All sorts of unclean animals were inside it. A voice from heaven told Peter to kill and eat some of them. He said no, and the voice told him several times to stop calling unclean the things God had sanctified.

The meaning of Peter's vision wasn't immediately apparent to him. He tried to interpret it while sitting on the rooftop. He pondered it while walking on the road toward the home of Cornelius, the Roman soldier who had sent for him. It took him until he was inside the door, and only then did he see the connection. God didn't want Peter to consider the Gentiles unclean any longer. In fact, he wanted him to go into this foreigner's home, preach the gospel to him, and in all likelihood eat foods that had previously been off limits for the Jews. (While Jesus had declared all foods clean in Mark 7:14-19, Peter's strong negative response to the vision seems to suggest he wasn't in the habit of eating those foods which the Law forbade.)

Refusing to eat with the Gentiles had the power to make

them feel like second-class citizens. This was a hard lesson for Peter to learn. The apostle Paul shared what happened in the church at Antioch in Galatians 2:11-21. Peter had come from Jerusalem and was regularly eating with the Gentiles, but when some of the more strict Jewish Christians from James showed up, he began to separate himself from them. Paul rebuked him for his hypocrisy, reminding him that salvation is by faith and not by following Jewish dietary laws.

While you and I may not feel compelled to observe the strict food laws of the Old Testament, you undoubtedly have a strong affinity for the foods you have grown up enjoying in your home culture. This is natural. You need to keep in mind, however, if you go to another country as a missionary, the people in that place have their own beloved foods. It won't help you should you look disdainfully at those foods, refusing to eat them. If you act that way, you will offend and hurt people. They might even feel like you are calling them unclean!

I was thankful when I first came to Vanuatu. Adjusting my eating habits to include local foods wasn't hard to do. (The exception is *kava*, which I mentioned earlier.) It wasn't difficult because I found the diet rich in organic fruits and vegetables. I was able to purchase fresh fish, beef, chicken, and goat. Flour, milk powder, sugar, ketchup, and other staple foods familiar to me and my wife were also available.

While transitioning to a Vanuatu diet wasn't difficult, there were funny moments. Let me share several of those stories with you.

One of the favorite meals in Vanuatu is called *laplap*. This dish is made with ground up manioc, yams, taro, sweet potatoes, or bananas. Once the root crop is ground up, it gets mixed with coconut cream. Often times spinach will be added. If the person preparing it has some fresh meat, he might put that in, too. This mixture gets wrapped in green leaves and cooked over hot stones. The result is a tasty tuber pudding.

I was sitting one afternoon with some friends enjoying this Vanuatu cuisine. As I ate it, I noticed something dark orange in the middle. I asked curiously, "What is this?" I was surprised when they told me it was pig blood that had been cooked into it.

One memorable meal occurred while I was backpacking around Southeast Tanna in 2003 in order to check it out as a potential place to work. A hospitable man and his wife invited me to set up my tent in their yard. When I finished, they called me into a dimly lit hut where they ate near an open fire. They gave me a plate full of vegetables. On top of the heap was a long, white, roasted grub worm as thick as my thumb and about four inches long.

A couple minutes into the meal, the man looked at my plate. I had been eating the vegetables first, trying to avoid the inevitable. "Have you ever had *pwir* before?" he asked.

I lifted the strange insect. It had folds in it that reminded me of the Michelin Man, the marshmallow-like cartoon character I had seen in old tire commercials growing up. I kept a poker face. "No, I've never had one of these before," I said.

The two of them sat staring, begging me with their eyes to taste it.

I took a large bite and smiled. It actually didn't taste bad; it was a bit like roasted pork. As I chewed it, the man and his wife began to laugh and nod approvingly at one another. I managed to get the whole thing down and had the distinct feeling I had made two new friends in the process.

Another humorous moment occurred several months later after we had moved into the village. A neighbor brought me a small piece of meat he had roasted before drinking *kava*.

"Missi Erik," he said, "I want you to try this."

"What is it?" I asked.

My neighbor laughed. "That's cat," he said. "Do they eat cat where you are from?"

Not wanting to appear apprehensive, I took a bite. I went on to explain my countrymen don't make a habit of eating their feline friends, but I told him I appreciated the chance he gave me to try this coveted dish.

Around the same time another neighbor brought over a plate of food. In the midst of the vegetables he had placed a Dracula-like creature. I didn't need to be told it was a fruit bat. These nocturnal animals had become familiar to me. They had large eyes and made loud screeching sounds. Every afternoon I had watched them as they flew down from the mountaintop in search of ripe fruits to eat. I told the neighbor thanks and ate it.

Adjusting to a Vanuatu diet had humorous moments for me, but I need to be honest. While I enjoy many foods native to this country, I don't actually prefer *laplap* with blood in it, grub worms, cat, or fruit bat. In fact, I've only tried each of them a handful of times (cat only once) while living on Tanna. In all cases, I ate them because I felt that accepting Tannese food, whatever it was, would help me develop relationships. It has certainly done that, not only in my own life, but especially in the lives of my children.

My children came to Tanna when our oldest was only five years old, and we gave them a lot of freedom to play with their village friends. These children soon taught my kids about Tanna and its various foods. They took them to their gardens and showed them how to plant and harvest root crops. They taught them how to roast a root crop over a small fire, scraping away the skin with shells from the beach. They showed them how to find grub worms in rotten trees. They cut sticks for them to throw at fruit bats. They made them slingshots and bows with arrows to shoot birds, spears to pierce crawdads, and small cane poles to catch fish. They also taught my kids how to prepare virtually every consumable part of an animal, an important skill in an environment where meat is rarely eaten. The animal's head, feet, stomach, intestines, lungs, kidneys, and even the bone marrow, they are all fair game on Tanna. And my children grew up eating it all with their friends.

When my children entered puberty, they quickly began to get taller than most of the shorter-in-stature Melanesian kids around them. Sometimes I would take them to Lenakel, and we would run into neighbors who only saw them occasionally. These friends would look up and down at my children while squeezing their shoulders. "Look at how fast they have grown up!" they would say, smiling proudly at me. "I think it's all the taro root they are eating, huh!" Often times they would go on to ask about our gardens and what we had planted in them that year.

Planting food, harvesting food, consuming food, conversing about food, and joyfully exchanging food are a major part of our lives on Tanna. While it hasn't always been easy or comfortable, intentionally participating in all these activities fosters warmth and acceptance. It has also proved to me again and again the truthfulness of what I was told many years before by a wise professor. "If you love me," he said, "you will love my food."

CHAPTER ELEVEN

AXIOM SEVEN — AVOID BEING ETHNOCENTRIC

Avoid being ethnocentric. The word ethno- comes from Greek *ethnos*. In the New Testament this word is used to refer to the nations — i.e. the Gentiles (Summers, 175). In English we use it to refer to people of the same race or nationality who share a distinctive culture. Centric refers to remaining centered in something.

An ethnocentric person is someone who stays centered in his own cultural milieu. He believes the customs practiced by the ethnic group or nation he is a part of are superior to the customs of others. When he encounters other cultures, he complains unhappily about the practices in them he finds unpleasant or different. If he's in a position of influence, he might try to impose his own cultural norms upon the people in that foreign culture. In a worst case scenario he might even try to eliminate those people and their customs altogether. (Genocide is the most extreme expression of ethnocentrism.)

People from industrialized nations visiting underdeveloped ones are often unashamedly ethnocentric. This is because their home countries have things like highly developed political and educational systems, tested medical procedures, military strength, and often a history of Christian truth. This gives them a sense of material, intellectual, and spiritual superiority.

This sense of superiority often creates arrogance which they cannot hide. You can imagine the kind of thing I'm talking about. The lines are long at the airport. The foreigner is used to efficiency. He gets impatient and vents his anger in public. The bank doesn't accept Visa, but the foreigner expects the quickness of a drive through and an ATM. He ends up swearing at the bank teller. The price of gas is $7.00 USD a gallon. The foreigner is used to half that price and so he accuses the guy pumping his gas of being a thief. The foreigner gets together with his expat friends, and the whole time all he can do is complain about how lazy the people in this backward country seem because they close shop from 11:30 until 1:30 every afternoon. He notices cockroaches crawling in his rented room. "Don't they have pest control!" he fumes. He smells piles of garbage being burned on the street outside. "Don't they have a dump!" he grumps. He can't understand why all the vehicles on the road are blaring ancient Reggae tunes from Bob Marley. "Wasn't that man buried a long time ago?" he wonders. The vehicles spew black smoke. "Don't they have pollution laws here?" he sputters. If he goes to the grocery store, he complains. The same is true at the hospital, government offices, and local restaurants. Everywhere he finds fault. Why? Because it's different than his beloved home culture.

Christian missionaries past and present aren't immune to this sort of angry, ethnocentric complaining. I was reminded of this recently while reading the memoirs of Agnes Watt. As I mentioned previously, she was the Presbyterian missionary who worked with her husband in Southeast Tanna from 1869 until her death in 1894.

Her writings have encouraged me countless times, especially since Michele and I feel we have joined into the work they began long ago. Yet Agnes couldn't hide her ethnocentrism.

She disliked the way the Tannese painted their faces. She said, "Their features, as a rule, are pleasing, and, were it not for the paint, they would compare favorably with other and higher races (Watt, 105). She didn't appreciate the attire of Tannese men. "The clothing of the men is so minute that I forbear to describe it. Yet they strut about in their disgusting costume . . . as though their own style of dress was of the highest order" (106). She described the bamboo-thatch homes of the Tannese as "the most wretched that one can well imagine" (106). She complained about the schedule of labor on Tanna, saying, "For four months they are busy in their plantations; the other eight are spent in idleness and wantonness" (110).

While Agnes displayed an ethnocentric attitude in the above examples, it's important to be fair. After all, she said those things during her first year on Tanna while undoubtedly struggling with culture shock. She would speak more positively of the Tannese seventeen years later:

> I live for Tanna (indeed many think I have Tanna on the brain), and will die for it, if need be. Can you wonder that we love the Tannese? Although they have opposed the gospel until they have become a proverb and a byword, and have by their waywardness sorely tried our faith, yet they are a most affectionate people (284).

Like Agnes who came before, I have struggled with my own ethnocentric feelings while living on Tanna. That's because many of the customs my Tannese friends practice are so different than what I became used to while growing up in America.

Take for example their marriage practices. My first exposure to Tannese marriage customs came shortly after our arrival in the village. I went over to get acquainted with a young man named Jack. It was late afternoon. He led me to a small veranda he had built in the middle of his yard. A nice breeze was rustling the trees. The cicadas were chirping. As we talked, Jack began to ask my opinion.

"Misi Erik. I've stolen a woman from a village by the sea. Her name is Lizzy. We are living together in my house. We like each other very much. But her father and mother do not approve. What do you think?"

Stolen a girl, I thought. *Hmm.* "Well, Jack, I can't say I think it's good. I think you should respect her parents' wishes." Then sensing there must be more to it, I continued, "Why did you steal her?"

"We really like one another. We both begged her parents, but they said she must marry and go back to her mother's village. But she doesn't like any of her cousins."

Her cousins? That sounds strange. I inquired further, and Jack began to explain Tannese marriage customs to me. When the Tannese boy or girl is growing up, he or she already knows the eligible group from which a spouse may come. This group is made up of first cousins. The main consideration is whether or not the cousin is the offspring of the same-sex or opposite-sex sibling of the child's parent.

Consider a young Tannese girl. She's not allowed to marry the sons of her father's brothers or her mother's sisters. They are her brothers. The sons of her mother's brothers or her father's sisters, however, are potential marriage partners.

The Tannese not only marry their first cousins, they marry very young. I've seen a girl not yet sixteen given in marriage to her mother's brother. Within a year her first baby came. Another came a year later, but it didn't survive outside the womb.

Americans don't marry their first cousins. That's too close in their family tree. Americans don't marry young. The expectation is that boys and girls will be at least eighteen when they make that commitment. For this reason when I first encountered Tannese marriage customs I thought they were bad. I wanted to complain and speak disparagingly about them. Yet doing that would have been ethnocentric. Marrying one's first cousins at a young age isn't wrong. It's simply different.

This idea of something being different but not necessarily wrong has been helpful to me. Whenever I begin to feel ethnocentric emotions rising in me in response to a foreign practice, I've learned to stop and ask questions before complaining. Is this custom wrong? Does the Bible forbid it explicitly or in principle? When the answer is no, I try to hold my tongue.

The missionary should be sensitive to the ethnocentric tendency in his own heart and try to avoid the negative expressions of it. If he allows his ethnocentric feelings to come out, his behavior will ruin relationships. His colleagues on the field won't want to be around him because of his sour attitude. His complaining will also repel the people he was sent to serve. They will tire quickly listening to him carry on in an arrogant manner about how things are done in his home culture.

Does this mean the missionary should always be silent when

he observes foreign practices he finds undesirable? This is not the case. If the custom in question is something the Bible forbids, the missionary should feel free to speak against it. Several examples from the past come to mind.

In China they used to bind women's feet. This was a debilitating, widespread practice that prevailed in that country from the tenth century until the mid-twentieth century. When a girl was between 5 and 7 years old, when the bones were still flexible, her feet would begin to be bound tightly. The bones would grow abnormally, causing deformity. The foot of a full-grown woman who had had her feet bound would have been only about three inches long! This was the ideal length and was considered attractive to men. "For a thousand years of Chinese history, foot-binding branded a person's gender, sex, beauty, and class (Ping, 226).

This practice was abusive and degrading to women. It was stopped in China, together with many other social ills contrary to the Bible, because of pressure that was first applied by concerned Christians and missionaries.

> Christian organizations had been key players in the diffusion of progressive social ideals, such as anti-foot-binding movement, which began with a group of sixty Christian women in Xiamen in 1874. The movement was taken up by the Women's Temperance Movement founded in 1883, which also opposed opium ... prostitution, and the selling of daughters. In addition, these ideas were advocated by missionaries ... (Goossaert and Palmer, 70).

When William Carey went to India in 1793, he labored there

for forty years. To his credit, he tried not to be ethnocentric. "He had respect for the Indian culture, and he never tried to import Western substitutes as so many missionaries who came after him would seek to do" (Tucker, Kindle Ed. 2769-2772). While he wanted to appreciate the Indian culture, this didn't keep him from speaking out against immoral practices like widow burning and infanticide (Tucker, Kindle Ed. 2768-2769).

In my own ministry on Tanna, I've often spoken publicly against common immoral practices. For example, in sermons I've talked about the wrongness of fornication and adultery, drug addiction, domestic violence, and other harmful practices. I've done this while pointing people to the forgiveness and freedom available in Christ. I've also felt compelled at times to speak against several widespread, animistic practices, like the practice of divination, or the practice of discussing in a non-Christian way who was responsible for death. (The Tannese always meet one week after a person dies and discuss who killed him. Normally it's attributed to black magic or the breaking of tribal customs.)

In conclusion, if you plan to be a missionary overseas, be prepared. You will encounter many things which will seem different to you. Perhaps they will make you feel uncomfortable. The natural tendency will be for you to view those things through the grid of your own cultural glasses, finding fault with the foreign while feeling a sense of pride in the familiar. That is one form of ethnocentrism.

You must guard against this tendency, recognizing that many cultural customs are morally neutral. They aren't right or wrong. They are simply different. You must learn to live with what is different without constantly complaining in a superior tone. On the other hand, when you encounter practices that are clearly wrong, you should feel free to speak against them in a gentle manner, pointing people toward what the Bible says.

CHAPTER TWELVE

AXIOM EIGHT — LEARN TO LAUGH AT YOURSELF

The Presbyterian church my family regularly attends while on Tanna had been collecting nickel-and-dime offerings for ten years. Slowly but surely they used those funds to build a new cement-block church building on the old mission station. When they finished it in the middle of 2012, they were filled with both gratitude and a sense of accomplishment. This was their building, the result of their own hard work and God's provision. They wanted to celebrate and have a dedication service. Invitations were sent out to people all over the island. People from every denomination were asked to come and present choir items.

Everyone in the congregation was given a part to play. Some would prepare the grounds beforehand. Others would give speeches. A large number would kill, dress, and cook three cows along with over one-hundred kilos of rice with local foods. I was given a role to play as well.

Since I was the only Caucasian missionary on hand, the committee asked me to help depict the arrival of the first missionaries. They wanted me to hold a Bible in the air while coming ashore in a boat. The male youth group members would dress up in leaves, painting their faces like fierce, cannibalistic warriors. With spears and clubs in their hands, they would act angry and antagonistic as I walked up the beach. (This was a drama based on popular imagination. It wasn't historically accurate. Yet I agreed to help anyway.)

The day for the celebration finally arrived. Several hundred people showed up early in the morning. The drama was the first thing on the agenda. The honored guests, including several government officials and influential people from the Department of Education, were asked to stand close to the beach and watch. Others crowded around behind them.

As they began to make their way to their spots, I got in the boat and was taken out to sea. After waiting beyond the reef for several minutes, the signal was given by a man on the shore, and we started moving slowly toward land. I stood erect at the front of the boat, looking confident and proud, holding a Bible high in the air. Imagine the Statue of Liberty with torch in hand and you get the picture.

Then something horrible happened. The boat hit a small swell, I lost my balance, the Bible flew from my grip, and the next thing I knew I was on my back, my feet the only noticeable body parts sticking up for the honored guests and the rest of the crowd to marvel at. I quickly rolled over, found the Bible, hopped up, and resumed my previous statue stance.

When I stepped ashore, several people had tears in their eyes. I wanted to imagine those tears were being shed on account of the memory of the sacrifices the early missionaries had made to come work on Tanna. However, I really had no way of knowing. The crowd had witnessed my clumsiness. Perhaps they were crying from laughter!

Thankfully the rest of the drama went off without a hitch. Several members from the youth group came running at me. Some pinched my skin and smelled my clothes. Others poked me with their spears. I shouted that I wanted to see the chief. As he approached, I held the Bible out. I told him I had a book that brought a message of peace. Did he want it? He agreed and began leading me toward his village. The drama was finished.

I got in line to follow the leaders back to the mission station. My clothes were wet and dirty from my previous spill in the bottom of the boat. As I walked, I did what every missionary must learn to do. I laughed at myself and stopped being concerned about what the people might or might not think of me.

Learning to laugh at myself was something I had learned to do early on the mission field. It was necessary for me to gain this skill because when I first arrived I was ignorant of the culture and the language. As a result, I often acted and spoke in inappropriate ways. Had I taken every mistake personally, getting emotionally preoccupied with what people thought about me because of it, I wouldn't have been able to function normally. I found it much more productive to simply laugh at myself for the blunder, learn from it, and then move on.

The most memorable, embarrassing mistake I ever made arose from my ignorance of animals and how they procreate. We had just gotten settled in our village on Tanna. I woke up one morning and went outside. I was met by a group of dogs growling and snapping at one another. When they saw me, all but two of them ran away. The two dogs that were left stood tail-to-tail, looking ruefully at me. How

133

was I supposed to know they were mating? I had grown up in the city, after all, and all my pets had been neutered. Anyway, I proceeded to make a spectacle of myself by chasing those two poor, inseparable creatures across the whole village. In plain view of all my national friends, I ran frantically, throwing sticks and stones while yelling, "Go away!" Needless to say, I was horrified when a language helper later informed me about the birds and the bees of a canine variety.

I also had embarrassing moments when I didn't understand common gestures. In America, when you want to acknowledge something, you either nod your head or say yes. On Tanna the people raise their eyebrows to communicate the affirmative. Imagine you are a Tannese guest eating at an American's home. In the middle of the meal your host asks you, "Do you like the pizza?" You acknowledge it by raising your eyebrows. Your friend stares dumbly at you and asks a second time, "So, do you like the pizza?" Again you acknowledge with your eyebrows. Only this time you smile wide. Then he asks you a third time the same question. Very annoying, huh? This scenario was common until I realized raising the eyebrows wasn't signaling surprise or suspicion but rather an affirmative answer.

The most common mistakes that caused embarrassment came with language learning. One morning I had gone down to the ocean for a workday at the church. The men were carrying timber while the women sat inside the mission station weaving mats and cooking food. I was shouldering several pieces of wood with another man. As we approached the women, he whispered a message to me.

"Misi Erik. *Iou ierman.* When we go past the women, say that to them."

I didn't want to disappoint. So when we got close to the ladies,

I smiled at them and said, *"Iou ieren."*

This caused laughter and several stupefied looks. My friend shouldering the load with me said, "No, no. *Iou ierman, ierman.* You are supposed to tell them you are a man. You told them you are a lobster."

On another occasion a friend came to visit me. I was pleased to see him and smiled wide. "Eh, hey, my friend!" I said.

He looked at me with alarm.

"What is it?" I asked.

"Why did you say that?" he replied.

"What?" I wondered, clearly baffled.

My friend then informed me that the word *eihi* is a very bad swear word. That's what he had understood when I greeted him by saying, "Eh, hey..."

Going to a different country to learn a new language and culture is an activity filled with challenges. One of those challenges is embarrassing situations. Falling on one's face in front of a crowd, acting ignorantly, misunderstanding common gestures, and making mistakes while learning language can cause emotional distress. Therefore, it's important for the missionary to learn to laugh at himself and take such situations in stride.

CHAPTER THIRTEEN

AXIOM NINE — KEEP YOUR MARRIAGE STRONG

It was early 1997. Michele and I were engaged. With our wedding only a few months away, our romantic affections were ablaze. I could think of no one but her, and she couldn't find time for anyone but me. Indeed, during those sweet days of engagement we took every available opportunity to be together, which is why we were sitting with one another one morning during the chapel hour on Moody's campus.

I don't recall many chapel services from 16 years ago, but I do recall this one. It made quite an impression on me. The main speaker was a popular marriage counselor. On this occasion he preached to the student body about the danger of going into marriage with unreal expectations.

When the service was over, Michele and I continued with our day. I went to my classes. She went to hers. We met again in the evening to study. We weren't together long before Michele sensed something was bothering me.

"Erik, what's the matter?" she asked.

"I didn't really appreciate chapel this morning. That's all."

"What was wrong with it?" she wondered.

"It didn't bother you, too?"

"No. I thought it was good."

"Hmm," I said. "I wonder how his wife must feel about him traveling around telling young people they can expect to fall out of love?"

While I've never fallen out of love with my wife, I've come to appreciate through the ups and downs of marriage what that counselor was trying to do. He was making an effort to inject just a bit of realism into my young, idealistic mind. Over the years I've learned that marriage is hard work and a strong marriage is essential for a missionary.

What does a strong marriage look like? Two people who have a strong marriage are faithful to one another. They aren't engaged in unfaithful behavior with the opposite sex in their thoughts, emotions, verbally, or physically. They also have healthy habits of communication and conflict resolution. The principles that govern their speech and actions toward one another are love, respect, and reverence for Christ. They live consistently by these principles in the power the Holy Spirit provides.

All Christians should endeavor to keep their marriages strong. The primary reason is it pleases God. He designed marriage to be a picture of Christ and his Church (Eph. 5:32). This is why he places a high priority on couples treating one another in a Christ-exalting manner. He has such a high regard for husbands and wives relating properly that he will stop listening to their prayers if they don't (Mal. 2:13-16; 1 Pet. 3:7).

While all Christians should keep their marriages strong to please God, there is another reason as well. A strong marriage is a powerful witness. It shines like a beacon in a world full of marriages that don't work as they should. It says to men and women who are emotionally exhausted by marital problems that there is a better way that Jesus Christ offers them.

The Lord knows that my friends in Vanuatu, and Tanna specifically, need to see such a light. A recent World Bank Development Report on Gender Equality and Development suggested that between 60 and 70 percent of woman in the Pacific nations of Kiribati, the Solomon Islands, and Vanuatu are victims of some form of domestic violence (Worldbank). Sadly, my family and I have witnessed this again and again.

Domestic disputes on Tanna are a regular part of life. Some disputes are out of the ordinary, the kind of thing you might read about in a magazine that publishes the sensational. You can imagine the headlines:

Infertile Wife Climbs Tree & Jumps to Her Death

Jealous Husband Kills Wayward Wife With Axe

Angry Wife Castrates Sleeping Husband with Machete

Michele and I have never actually witnessed those events. We have only heard them whispered at times. When we heard, we prayed they were exaggerations.

While we haven't witnessed the sensational, we have often been involved pastorally in the mundane, common, and less violent conflicts between husbands and wives. (I said "less" meaning no one died.) Let me share several of their stories.

A young, newly married couple were in their yard one afternoon. The wife was in her last trimester of pregnancy. She and her friends were playing cards and laughing together. The girl's husband didn't want her playing cards and told her how he felt. She ignored him. He waited several minutes and said it again. She still didn't listen. Exasperated, the husband took a long post and poked his wife violently in the stomach, inducing labor. I stood by later while the village chiefs asked what had motivated the husband. He replied, "I told her to stop playing cards, but she didn't respect my words."

A close friend in the village always seemed to be having marital problems for the first several years after our arrival. The first time the wife ran away to her mother's home it was because her husband had threatened her verbally. After much coaxing she came back because he had kept their three children. A couple years later they got into a fight about something inconsequential. He clobbered her over the head with a stone while they were in the garden. She was bloody and sobbing when he ran away. The result was a six-month separation, infidelity by both the husband and the wife, and then a reconciliation later.

"Missi Erik," the man confessed just after the incident in the garden, tears running down his cheeks. "As I fled, all I could think about was Cain killing his brother Abel."

One husband kicked his wife hard in the face with a steel-toed boot. Today she has a perpetual scar from just above her eyebrow halfway down her cheek. She received this abusive treatment because she spoke disrespectfully to him in front of the other men.

Another middle-aged man told his family he was going to his garden to cut a stick. His wife was going to be coming back from the market soon. She had been gone too long. He was going to whip her. Since both he and his wife were very close to our family, I asked him to come over when I heard about his plan. We had just finished translating First Corinthians. I read to him the passage about love in chapter thirteen. He listened quietly while looking at the floor. After I prayed with him, he looked up. "Missi Erik, I confess," he said. "My plan was to beat her when she came home. But now I've left those thoughts completely." (In the end the wife came home and told him she had stayed in town to purchase Christmas gifts with the money she had made at the market.)

One young girl we watched grow up married a young man and moved to the other side of the island. The first time her husband beat her it was with a tree limb. Though bruised on her back, she forgave him. A year later he cut her scalp and forearm with a machete. A friend took her to the clinic where she got stitched up. Unlike many women she took her husband to court for his crimes. (Vanuatu actually has a strict law now that forbids this kind of violence, but we have found more often than not such matters get settled at the community level on Tanna.) The court decided for this first offense they had to make a swap, each giving the other the equivalent of $20 USD and a pig. The husband was told if he did it again he would go to jail.

Sometimes the domestic disputes didn't end in violence, but they were nonetheless tragic. One example comes to mind.

I was in our house one evening when a mother-tongue translator came to the door. He asked me to come to the other side of the village. A young, recently-married man had just tried to hang himself. He had been hanging from the end of the rope for a short time when he was discovered. By the time they got him out of the noose, he had stopped breathing. Thankfully, they were able to revive him. After convulsions, vomiting, and a late night trip to the local aid post, he recovered. I visited him the following morning. His new wife was sitting next to him as he was lying on his bed. I tried to get him to tell me what had filled him with such hopelessness. He didn't tell me then, but I found out later it was a domestic dispute.

Why have I shared all these abusive and tragic stories with you? It wasn't to make you think the Tannese are worse than anyone else. We are all human and capable of behaving in the same unhealthy ways displayed in these stories. I've shared these things with you because I want you to feel with me the crisis in our particular situation that provides some of the impetus for Michele and I to keep our marriage strong and be that aforementioned witness through our actions. We want our Tannese friends who have domestic problems to see in us that there is a godly way for married couples to relate to one another.

While Michele and I always feel the incentive to keep our marriage strong, it would be dishonest to suggest that it's easy. It's not, and we often fail. For this reason forgiveness is essential. We've also learned to recognize the things that repeatedly cause conflict in our marriage.

Failing to show appropriate affection can cause conflict. If a husband or a wife isn't having his or her emotional and physical desires met at home, whether home is a remote house on a solitary hill or an apartment in a large city, the temptation becomes strong for them to find those desires met somewhere else.

The challenge Michele and I experience in this area arises from cultural taboos against public displays of affection and a general lack of privacy. As I mentioned before, Tannese men and women don't show affection to one another when others are watching. It doesn't matter if they are married or not. It just doesn't happen. This means I can't hold hands with my wife in public. I can't put my arm around her. There are no kisses on the cheek to say I love you. That kind of affection must be shown behind closed doors.

Yet even behind closed doors it can be difficult to express affection. Privacy is a major problem. Little house. Thin bamboo walls. Curious kids in the yard, and our own children always nearby. It all leads to feeling like one is living in a fishbowl. If Michele and I aren't careful, this lack of affection can easily lead to negative thoughts and feelings that can weaken our marriage.

Feeling unproductive can cause conflict. When Michele and I were preparing to come overseas, she took graduate-level courses in literacy. She assumed she would come to Vanuatu and learn the language and culture and have opportunities to be involved in that life-changing work. Once we arrived in the village, caring for our children was a fulltime job. Often times she would get frustrated. "You need to take these kids for a couple hours so I can go learn the language. If you are not going to help me, then I'm ready to go back to America. Everything I'm doing here I can do easier there!"

I'm thankful for wise friends. Early on in this work several of them counseled me, stressing how important it was going to be for me to support my wife by helping her feel productive in ministry outside the home. I listened to their words and took the kids often. Michele went on to speak South Tannese. Over the years she has taught vernacular education in the local schools and had a fruitful ministry in addition to her duties at home.

Expectations about what material possessions are really

necessary for life and ministry can cause conflict. We knew a man and his wife who loved the Lord and went into missions. Both of them had grown up in Southern California in upper middleclass homes. The husband had enjoyed many "toys" as a young adult, things like motorcycles and assorted gadgets and tools that made life comfortable and easy. When he went overseas, he wanted to have those things in his remote village home. His wife, on the other hand, was happy with much less and was concerned about what all that "stuff" would communicate to the locals around them who had far less. In the end they both had to compromise. She agreed to certain purchases for his sake, and for her sake he refrained from buying some things he would have liked.

Feeling physically or socially isolated can cause conflict. A female colleague living with her husband in a situation similar to the one Michele and I live in made the following observations:

> Out in the village, we mostly have only each other to talk with in any deep and intimate way. Even close cross-cultural friends cannot generally relate to the particular stresses we face as Westerners living far from our comfort zones. So we build up a lot of stress and don't have (in my case) female friends to "let off steam" with or talk things through with in a constructive way. So the normal stresses of everyday living get built up into something more than they should be. This is compounded by having small children and not much energy left at the end of the day to spend together. In short, I find that I "like" my husband a lot better when I'm around other people of my own culture, and he finds that he is not called upon to meet all my emotional and relational needs as much

when we are, say, in the United States among family and friends, as when we are isolated in the village.

Stress caused by moving all the time can cause conflict. Our family moves from island to island a couple times a year. We normally go on furlough to the United States every four years. This movement causes stress. Who should we visit on furlough? What needs to be packed and what can be left behind? How long should we stay in one place? Questions like these need to be discussed, and the answers need to be agreed upon. There are often long lines at the airport, delayed planes, and many more things like these that cause tension.

Michele and I were packing our suitcases one morning after a refreshing, year-long furlough. Our thoughts were torn between two lives, the one we had been living in our home country and the one we were returning to in Vanuatu. We didn't relish the idea of leaving family and friends again. Yet there was a job to be done. We felt the tug of that commitment, as well as the strong pull of the many friends and workmates on the field who had become like genuine family to us.

While standing over those suitcases, all those feelings were inside our hearts, causing stress. Michele suggested I pack another pair of pants. I told her I didn't need them. Soon we were locked in a heated exchange full of mean, hurtful comments. After several minutes of this my wife graciously said, "Erik, let's stop this." That defused the conflict. We apologized to one another, admitting the familiar stress we both felt from having to move again. We went on to spend some time praying together, asking God to help us.

Issues surrounding money can cause conflict. Learning to navigate through financial questions with your spouse can be a bit like walking through a minefield, requiring wisdom and grace. Who is going to manage the budget? Who's going to carry the credit cards? What's an appropriate amount for generous family members to give? When is it too much? When is it acceptable to ask others from financial help? Are we going to make long-term investments in anything like a home or property? Michele and I ask questions like these all the time, and if we aren't careful and thoughtful, they can cause conflict.

While I've discussed many of the issues that can cause conflict in my marriage and in the marriages of my missionary friends, the truth of the matter is that conflict is a part of life, and therefore it's present in every home between every husband and wife. One of the things that distinguishes between couples with strong marriages and those with weak ones is the manner in which they deal with such strife.

Conflict resolution is something all people have learned. The lessons began when they were young while they lived with siblings and parents. Unfortunately, some people didn't learn healthy habits, and their marriages today reflect that. When others see the way they interact, they don't think of Christ and his Church. Instead, they see physical and/or verbal abuse.

When I was engaged to Michele, we were encouraged to get some premarital counseling. It was good advice. During the counseling sessions our pastor shared several truths about marriage from the Bible. He asked us many questions about our backgrounds and the expectations we had for our future together. He also recommended several books about marriage. These books impressed upon us the importance of things like being faithful and learning to communicate in a godly way. They discussed establishing healthy habits of conflict resolution early on in the dating and marriage relationship.

This chapter has been very brief, too brief to delve into all the aspects of a strong marriage. Yet it's a start. If you are not married yet, perhaps you should try to reinforce healthy habits of communication and conflict resolution in your life. Paying close attention to how you relate to your parents, siblings, and close friends can be helpful as you seek to do this. If you are engaged to be married, perhaps you should consider getting some premarital counseling. If you are already married and struggling with things like conflict resolution, perhaps you and your spouse would benefit from reading some Christian literature on the topic. Perhaps you should consider getting biblical counseling.

We live in a world where people dearly need to see marriages that glorify Christ and please God. For this reason Christian men and women, missionaries included, need to keep their marriages strong.

CHAPTER FOURTEEN

AXIOM TEN — TRUST IN GOD'S SOVEREIGNTY

The Bible teaches us that God has been reigning forever. The prophet Jeremiah spoke confidently of him as "the eternal King" (10:10). King David praised God, saying, "Your kingdom is an everlasting kingdom, and your dominion endures through all generations" (Ps. 145:13).

Not only is God the eternal King, but his rule encompasses all things. King David said in another place, "The Lord has prepared his throne in the heavens, and his kingdom rules over all" (Ps. 103:19).

The Lord Jesus affirmed this universal government of God over all things, things both small and great. He taught that it's God who clothes the lilies of the field (Matt. 6:26-30). He feeds the birds and watches over their death (Matt. 10:29). It is God who numbers and changes the color of people's hair (Matt. 5:36; 10:30). He sends the rain and caused the sun to rise (Matt. 5:45). He is also the one who gives human rulers their authority. This was a truth Pilate had overlooked, but our Lord reminded him of it (John 19.11).

The Bible's teaching about God's sovereignty is a broad topic, but McClain summed it up by citing James Orr:

> There is therefore recognized in Scripture . . . a natural and universal kingdom or dominion of God, embracing all objects,

persons, and events, all doings of individuals and nations, all operations and changes of nature and history, absolutely without exception (22).

It's important to remember that God has everything under his control. When a Christian understands this and believes it, it will help him cultivate quietness and trust in his heart. He will find a reason for hope in all circumstances. It will produce inner strength as he waits on the Lord to work all things together for the good of those who love him (Rom. 8:28).

If a Christian forgets that God is ruling over all the circumstances in his life, his lack of faith will create depression, hopelessness, a sense of failure, anxiety with fear, and other debilitating feelings. These emotions will grip his soul and cause him to struggle spiritually.

All Christians wrestle at times with these emotions. No one is exempt, including missionaries. That's why this axiom is so important: you should trust in God's sovereignty. Let me suggest several areas where the missionary needs to apply this truth.

GOD'S SOVEREIGNTY IN THE PAST

Missionaries overseas often live and work together in a community. And like any community, all the members in it will have their own unique backgrounds. Some might have come from a broken home. Others might have never felt the pain of divorce. Some might be second or third generation Christians whose parents and grandparents nurtured them and carefully instilled in them a biblical worldview. Others might be first generation Christians who didn't grow up in such a spiritually supportive environment. Some might have grown up feeling safe. Others might have experienced some kind of abuse. Some might have been well educated. Others might have been less so. Some might have known financial advantages growing up. Others might have experienced poverty.

Those Christians who have had a positive past, one that fills them with fond memories, will probably find it easy to trust that God was sovereign over their former circumstances. They know God is good, and they both see and feel that goodness when they look backwards.

It's often different for those with a troubled past. While they understand God is good, and also believe he is sovereign, if they are honest, they will admit that sometimes they wish he would have ruled over their situations differently. They might wonder why he didn't sovereignly choose to either effect or permit less painful outcomes in their lives.

Thinking this way isn't helpful. It causes you to become self-absorbed. You will begin to feel sorry for yourself. Perhaps you will begin to look jealously at your colleagues, wishing your past could have been like theirs. Your focus will be backward not forward, and you'll waste emotional energy on things you cannot change.

The apostle Paul's life has always encouraged me when I'm tempted to look backward and focus in an unhelpful way on my past. I can see in him a model for understanding the Christian life. It's a model that acknowledges God's sovereign design from beginning to end.

God had set Paul apart from birth (Gal. 1:15-16). However, he didn't immediately give Paul the Holy Spirit like he had done, for example, with John the Baptist (Luke 1:15). Instead, he allowed Paul to live many years as an unregenerate man. During that time Paul experienced many things that would shape him into the unique apostle he would later become. He also did many things he would look back on with sorrow. For example, he was self-righteous. He also persecuted the Church. When Paul finally came to faith, it was neither early nor late on God's sovereign timetable. It happened right on time, when it pleased God to graciously reveal his Son in Paul.

After God revealed Christ to Paul, Paul's perspective on life changed. He had a new focus. He only wanted to know Christ and be found in him with the righteousness given to him because of his faith. He wanted to suffer with Christ and attain to the resurrection of the dead. These things led him to leave his past in God's sovereign hands while looking toward the future. In Philippians 3:13-14 he said the following:

> Brothers, I do not consider myself yet to have taken hold of it. But one thing I do: Forgetting what is behind and straining toward what is ahead, I press on toward the goal to win the prize for which God has called me heavenward in Christ Jesus.

GOD'S SOVEREIGNTY IN THE PRESENT

The missionary needs to trust that God was sovereign over his past, but he also needs to trust in God's sovereignty when he makes decisions in the present. I'm not talking about sinful decisions. I'm not addressing daily decisions like the choosing of one breakfast cereal over another. While such choices aren't outside of God's providential care and control, I'm really addressing the larger choices the missionary must make, choices that require him to consider his options while praying in a more focused, intentional way.

Should I marry this person and go into the ministry? What country should I serve in? When should I go? What should the focus of my ministry be? Should I homeschool my kids or send them to boarding school? What's the most effective way to reach this group of people? Should I evacuate on account of a medical emergency? How should I respond to this political unrest? Is it time to move on from this ministry and get another job? Questions like these are regularly asked by missionaries.

Such questions need to be studied and prayed about. We need wisdom from God to come to a decision. Yet once we have settled on a course of action, our hearts should be comforted by the promise of God's sovereignty over our choices. King Solomon's words remind us, "In his heart a man plans his course, but the Lord determines his steps" (Prov. 16:9).

GOD'S SOVEREIGNTY OVER SALVATION

When I was a new Christian back in 1991, I was working one morning at LOVE Inc. in Fairbanks, Alaska. A woman in need called the hotline asking for a box of food. When I delivered it to her house, I stepped into her living room. Her husband was in the corner sitting in a recliner. His lifelong habit of chain smoking had reduced his body to skin and bones. Oxygen tubes hung from his nose and fed his cancer-filled lungs.

I shared the gospel with that decrepit old man. I made it as clear as I could, but he wasn't interested. In fact, he spoke arrogantly against the truth. He took the food and shooed me away.

The man's unbelief didn't deter me. I began frequenting his home. Every visit I would witness to him and ask him to believe in Christ. Every time he would shake his head and say he didn't want the Savior.

The time came when the cancer overwhelmed his body. He was dying, and I was given still one more chance to see him. He was in the hospital. Pain medication had made him groggy. I sat down next to his bed, said a prayer, and then went on to remind him one last time of Christ's salvation. I also warned him about hell's flames. Still he refused to budge, clinging tightly to his unbelief.

I don't know whether or not that man went on to have a thief-on-the-cross experience with Christ. I sincerely hope he did. What I do know, however, is I felt horrible when I left the hospital that afternoon. I felt like a failure. I thought to myself, *Perhaps the formula I used for presenting the gospel was wrong. Was I too pushy? Maybe I should have given him some relaxing Christian music to listen to while sitting in his bed. That might have softened him a bit, making him more responsive to the good news.*

Do you see anything wrong with that train of thought? I do. I wasn't appreciating that God is sovereign in salvation. He saves the sinner, not me! Because this is true, no amount of begging, cajoling, or emotional manipulation could have genuinely changed the man's heart. God's Spirit needed to blow, granting him repentance, new life, and all the justifying benefits of faith. If he sovereignly chose to refrain from moving in that way, nothing I did or said could change the dying man.

If the missionary fails to appreciate that saving sinners is ultimately God's work, he risks going through life feeling like a failure in ministry. He will be discouraged and sigh if no one seems interested in his efforts to reach them with the gospel. When his supporting churches write and ask him to fill out his monthly report, if his ministry isn't bearing lots of tangible fruit, he will puzzle uncomfortably over the question, "How many first time responses to the gospel have you seen?"

On the other hand, the missionary trusting that God is sovereign in salvation doesn't need to be discouraged. He knows both God's expectations and his own limitations. Does God want him to be faithful to the ministry he was sent to do? Yes. Does God want him to share the gospel faithfully and clearly at every opportunity? Absolutely! While the missionary does these things, he also recognizes he is only human. He might plant the seed of the gospel in the harvest field of a person's heart. He might water it, but it's God who makes it grow (1 Cor. 3:7).

GOD'S SOVEREIGNTY IN TRAUMATIC SITUATIONS

Several years ago a missionary family we know experienced trauma. They were packing their bags inside their apartment, preparing to return to Canada on furlough that morning. Suddenly they heard screaming outside. The father stepped onto the balcony and looked down with horror at his four-year-old daughter. She was being mauled by four menacing dogs. He leapt over the railing and rushed to his baby's side. Her scalp, legs, and arms were filled with large gashes that would take more than one hundred stitches to mend.

Another time this man's wife was driving a large truck back from a church activity. Twenty-plus children and adults were with her. She came to a notoriously dangerous hill on the outskirts of Port

Vila. As she cautiously drove down it, the brakes stopped working. She fought for control, making a final hairpin turn before the truck rolled onto its side and slid for several hundred feet.

I listened to them share their testimony once. They said Christians often say to them, "Satan must not like the work you are doing in Bible translation. Look at how he has been attacking your family."

The wife explained with tears that they really didn't know if it was Satan behind those terrible events. What they did know was that God was sovereign. They went on to praise him for his providential control. Their daughter's body had been violently torn, but God had spared her life. They were also grateful he had kept the dogs from mutilating her face. When the truck turned, the wife broke her collar bone. Others got bruises and scrapes. Yet God had done what one witness said had rarely happened before with such accidents on that hill. He had kept everyone alive, including an infant inside the cab. Those beloved friends have always been an example to me. They've shown me how to search for good in traumatic situations, trusting that God rules even during those horrible times.

GOD'S SOVEREIGNTY IN THE FUTURE

Most Christians, if they were asked what displeases God, would point to familiar actions God has said are offensive to him, things like idolatry, taking his name in vain, disobeying parents, murder, adultery, stealing, lying, and coveting. Most wouldn't include worrying in such a list. It's just such a common emotion, isn't it? Yet the Lord Jesus insisted in the Sermon on the Mount that worry is wrong (Matt. 6:25-34). He forbade it, insisting his people shouldn't spend their days anxious and preoccupied with tomorrow. God is sovereign, and he will take care of them and make sure they have what they need each day.

As a missionary I often battle this pestiferous emotion. That's because there's always something to worry about. I'm especially vulnerable when it comes to my children's health and education. I want to know they are physically strong and going to be equipped academically to survive in their passport country. It's easy for me to worry about money since making large, long term investments isn't possible. Where will I live on furlough? What car will I drive? What happens after this phase of ministry is finished? Questions like these can also cause distressing anxiety.

Jesus' disciples weren't immune to worrying about the future. Their concern about it came out once after Jesus had talked with a rich man who wanted eternal life (Mark 10:17-31). The man ended up going home with his worldly wealth intact, but he sadly remained spiritually bankrupt. As he left, Jesus pointed out to his disciples just how difficult it is for the wealthy to enter God's kingdom. It's easier for a camel to pass through the eyes of a needle! Then Peter spoke up for them all and asked what their futures held. After all, they had left everything to follow Christ.

> "I tell you the truth," Jesus replied, "no one who has left home or brothers or sisters or mother or father or children or fields for me and the gospel will fail to receive a hundred times as much in this present age (homes, brothers, sisters, mothers, children and fields–and with them, persecutions) and in the age to come, eternal life. But many who are first will be last, and the last first" (Mark 10:29-31)

With these words our Lord promised provision for his mission-minded people. They don't need to worry. They can trust him. This is easier for them to do if they will remember he was sovereign over their past. He is sovereign over the decisions they are making in the present. He is sovereign over salvation. Traumatic situations are under his control. Not only that, but their future remains firmly in his grip as well.

CHAPTER FIFTEEN

CONCLUSION – MISSIONS POSSIBLE!

It's appropriate that I'm sitting down to write the final chapter of this book today since this day was a conclusion of sorts for the translation project, too. After a solid week of reading from eight in the morning until four-thirty in the afternoon, a group of sixteen men and women from all around Southeast Tanna made it through the complete *Nafe* New Testament. It was the final read-thru, and now the manuscript, a ten-year labor of love, is ready for typesetting.

The last couple hours of our time together was full of God-honoring activity. I shared a short devotion, summing up all that we had read. Knowing there were people present who hadn't believed in Christ, I gave an invitation to accept him. We sang songs of praise. We joined hands, knelt down, and gave thanks to God. We asked him for his help with the remaining work that must be completed before the planned dedication next year.

Many people shared a few words before we closed. One man, a notoriously duplicitous (albeit hilarious) chief with two wives, shared in all seriousness what he felt. He said, "I came here and listened to this book. I've heard it before in *Bislama*. I've heard it in English, which comes from overseas, but I don't understand those languages. I will tell you the truth. The church in my village, we worship on the surface only. We don't really understand the meaning of what we are doing. This book (the *Nafe* New Testament) speaks clearly. We need this book to teach our children and grandchildren so they can understand which road they are on. They need to know if they are going to heaven or the place of fire."

Another young woman who had been instrumental in the translation process had to stand quiet for several moments before speaking since she was holding back her tears. When she composed herself, she went on to share her testimony.

She had grown up in a village located at the heart of the John Frum Movement. Shortly before our arrival on Tanna in 2003, she had married and moved to the village we would later call our home. Her heart was in darkness at that time. Then the translation project began. We invited her to be involved. She accepted and soon found herself wrestling with the Bible, trying to (a) understand the meaning, and (b) articulate it clearly in her own language. Through the process she saw God's light in Christ and was joyfully born again.

One day the young woman returned to her parents' village. "I've found something," she told them excitedly. Then she went on to share the gospel and urged her dad and mom to leave John Frum and trust in the Lord Jesus. She was disappointed when her father spoke harshly to her, but she didn't give up. She returned to her home and began to pray for them. When she visited her family some time later, her parents informed her that they had had a change of heart. They both had accepted Christ and had been baptized. The young woman was delighted that God had heard her prayers and answered.

As I sat quietly listening to what God's Spirit had been doing in people's hearts through the translated Scriptures, I unashamedly let my own tears roll down my cheeks. The translation process had been long and arduous for everyone involved. There had been so many challenges, too. So many times I had wanted to quit. Yet God had been faithful and supplied all we needed again and again.

I couldn't help but think back to a late night walk I had taken in Alaska back in 1992. I was so thrilled about the new life God had graciously given me in Christ. With that new life came a sense of hopeful possibility where before I had had no real sense of purpose in my life. The temperature was below zero. I was following a small footpath in the snow, crossing a baseball field en route to the control tower to work a mid-shift. I stopped for a moment, lifted my hands toward the sky, and then prayed, "Lord, I want to write a book someday. Lord, please let me write a book."

To this day I'm not sure where that prayer came from. No one in my family had been a writer. I hadn't been encouraged to compose literary pieces as a teenager. At any rate, had the Lord revealed to me on that cold night that I would indeed write a book someday, HIS BOOK, with the help of a dedicated translation team in a foreign language spoken on a remote island in the Pacific, I undoubtedly would have laughed like Sarah at the promise of Isaac's birth (Gen. 18:12). I would have said, "Surely that's not possible, is it, Lord? I'm just an average guy, after all!"

I'm happy to conclude in this final chapter that being engaged in such meaningful mission work is possible. Becoming a fulltime Christian missionary in order to work in God's harvest field overseas doesn't have to be for others. You can do it! You might not become a Bible translator like I did, but there are ministries all around the world that would benefit from your unique background and the gifts the Lord has given you.

I hope that reading my story has encouraged you to go. Remember Jesus' words in John 4:35-36:

> Do you not say, 'Four months more and then the harvest'? I tell you, open your eyes and look at the fields! They are ripe for harvest. Even now the reaper draws his wages, even now he harvests the crop for eternal life, so that the sower and the reaper may be glad together.

The need for workers is real, and the wages for labor precious. Men and women all around the world need to hear the good news of Jesus Christ. Will you be the one to take it to them?

As you finish this book, please take a moment to read the following prayer and pray it yourself if it reflects your feelings:

Father in Heaven,

The world is your harvest field. I want to be like the prophet Isaiah who said, 'Here am I, send me' (Is. 6:8). Fill me with your Spirit and keep me from sinful habits so that I can be the sort of person the apostle Paul told Timothy to be, a person set apart for honorable occasions, useful to the Master, and prepared for every good work (2 Tim. 2:21). As I prepare to go, help me be patient and fruitful in ministry. And when the time comes for me to leave my home, give me wisdom to live cross-culturally, and do through me, and those who will partner with me by praying and giving, immeasurably more than we ask or imagine, according to your power at work in us (Eph. 3:20). Do all these things so that the nations will come to recognize Christ's greatness. In Jesus' name. Amen

BIBLIOGRAPHY

Berkhof, Lois. "Systematic Theology." East Peoria: Versa Press, Inc., 1958.

Geisler, Norman L. & Howe, Thomas. "The Big Book of Bible Difficulties." Grand Rapids: Baker Books, 1992.

Goossaert, Vincent & Palmer, David. "The Religious Question in Modern China." Chicago & London: University of Chicago Press, 2011.

Lindstrom, Monty. "Cult and Culture: American Dreams in Vanuatu" in Pacific Studies Vol. IV, No. 2 Spring 1981. 101-123.

McClain, Alva. "The Greatness of the Kingdom." Winona Lake: BMH Books, 1974.

Miller, Graham, J. Live: A History of Church Planting in the New Hebrides. (Seven volumes) Sydney: Bridge Printery.

Paton, John G. "John G. Paton Missionary to the New Hebrides." Glasgow:(Banner of Truth Trust) Bell & Bain Ltd, 2002.

Sproul, R.C. "Chosen By God." Carol Stream: Tyndale House Publishers, Inc., 1986.

Summers, Ray. "Essentials of New Testament Greek." Nashville: Broadman & Holman Publishers, 1995.

Tucker, Ruth A. "From Jerusalem to Irian Jaya: A Biographical History of Christian Missions" 2011. Zondervan Publishing Company. Kindle Edition.

Turner, George. "Nineteen Years in Polynesia." London: John Snow, Paternoster Row, 1861.

Unger, Merrill F. "The New Unger's Bible Dictionary." Chicago: Moody Press, 1988.

Watt, Agnes C.P. "Twenty-Five Years' Mission Life on Tanna, New Hebrides." London: Houlston and Sons, 1896.

Wang, Ping. "Aching for Beauty: Footbinding in China." Minneapolis: University of Minnesota Press, 2000.

worldbank.org/en/news/2012/11/25/raising-awareness-of-violence-against-women-in-the-pacific. (2/2/2013)

Made in the USA
Charleston, SC
19 October 2015